move up

Pre-intermediate
Teacher's Book

B

Heinemann

Simon Greenall

Heinemann English Language Teaching
A division of Reed Educational and Professional Publishing Limited
Halley Court, Jordan Hill, Oxford OX2 8EJ

OXFORD MADRID ATHENS PARIS FLORENCE PRAGUE SÃO PAULO
CHICAGO MELBOURNE AUCKLAND SINGAPORE TOKYO IBADAN
GABORONE JOHANNESBURG PORTSMOUTH (NH)

ISBN 0 435 29866 6

Layout by eMC Design
Cover design by Stafford & Stafford

Author's acknowledgements
I am very grateful to all the people who have contributed towards the
creation of this book. My thanks are due to:
- All the teachers I have had the privilege to meet on seminars in
  many different countries and the various people who have
  influenced my work.
- Paul Ruben for producing the tapes, and the actors for their voices.
- The various schools who piloted the material.
- Simon Stafford for the stunning design of the book.
- James Hunter and Bridget Green for their careful attention to detail
  and their creative contribution.
- Clare Leeds for her careful management of the project.
- Helena Gomm for her patient and good-humored editorial input.
- And last, but by no means least, Jill, Jack, and Alex.

Acknowledgments
The authors and publishers would like to thank the following for their
kind permission to reproduce material in this book:
American Medical Association for an extract from an article "Report:
seat belts, helmets save lives and health costs" by Christina Kent in
the journal *American Medical News*, March 1 1996, Vol.39, Page 10.
Copyright © 1996.

While every effort has been made to trace the owners of copyright
material in this book, there have been some cases when the publishers
have been unable to contact the owners. We should be grateful to hear
from anyone who recognises their copyright material and who is
unacknowledged. We shall be pleased to make the necessary amend-
ments in future editions of the book.

Printed and bound in Great Britain by Athenaeum Press Ltd.

97 98 99 00 10 9 8 7 6 5 4 3 2 1

Contents

Introduction

Course Organization

Move Up is a general English course which will take adult and young adult learners of English from elementary level to advanced level. American English is used as the model for grammar, vocabulary, spelling, and pronun-ciation, but other varieties of English are included for listening and reading practice. The course components for each level are as follows:

For the student	For the teacher
Student's Book	Teacher's Book
Practice Book	Class cassettes
	Resource Pack
	Business Resource Pack

The Student's Book has twenty teaching lessons, four Fluency lessons, and four Progress Check lessons. After every five teaching lessons there is a Fluency lesson and a Progress Check lesson to review the language covered in the preceding teaching lessons and to present new language work relevant to the grammar, functions, and topics covered so far. Within the teaching lessons, the main grammar or language functions and the most useful vocabulary are presented in boxes that allow easy access to the principal language of the lesson. This makes the focus of the lesson clearly accessible for purposes of presentation and review. Each lesson will take about 90 minutes.

The **Class cassettes** contain all the listening and sounds work in the Student's Book.

The Practice Book has twenty practice lessons corresponding to the twenty teaching lessons in the Student's Book. The Practice Book extends work done in class with the Student's Book by providing further practice in grammar, vocabulary, reading, and writing. The activities are designed for self-access work and can be used either in the class or as self-study material. Each lesson will take between 45 and 60 minutes.

The Teacher's Book contains a presentation of the course design, methodological principles, as well as detailed teaching notes. It also includes two photocopiable tests. The teaching notes for each lesson include a step-by-step guide to teaching the lesson, a discussion of some of the difficulties the learners may encounter, and more detailed methodological issues arising from the material presented. The Practice Book Answer Key is in the Teacher's Book and may be photocopied.

The Resource Packs provide additional teaching material to practice the main language points of the teaching lessons. *Move Up* is designed to be very flexible in order to meet the very different requirements of learners. There is a Resource Pack for learners of general English and a Business Resource Pack for learners with language requirements of a more professional nature.

Each pack contains a wide variety of communicative prac-tice activities in the form of photocopiable worksheets with step-by-step Teacher's Notes on the back. There is at least one activity for each lesson in the Student's Book, and the activities can be used to extend a core teaching lesson of 90 minutes from the Student's Book with an average of 30 minutes of extra material for use in the classroom. They can also be used to review specific structures, language, or vocabulary later in the course.

As well as step-by-step Teacher's Notes for each activity, each Resource Pack includes an introduction which explains how to use the worksheets and offers tips on how to get the most out of the activities.

Course Design

The course design is based on a broad and integrated multi-syllabus approach. It is broad in the sense that it covers grammar and language functions, vocabulary, reading, listening, speaking, writing, and sounds explicitly, and topics, learner training, and socio-cultural competence implicitly. It is integrated in that each strand of the course design forms the overall theme of each lesson. The lessons always include activities focusing on grammar and language functions, and vocabulary. They also include reading, listening, speaking, writing, and sounds. The inclusion of each strand of the syllabus is justified by its communicative purpose within the activity sequence. The methodological principles and approaches to each strand of course design are discussed below.

Methodological Principles

Here is an outline of the methodological principles for each strand of the course design.

Grammar and Language Functions

Many teachers and learners feel safe with grammar and language functions. Some learners may claim that they want or need grammar, although at the same time suggest that they don't enjoy it. Some teachers feel that their learners' knowledge of grammar is demonstrable proof of language acquisition. But this is only partly true. Mistakes of grammar are more easily tolerated than mistakes of vocabulary, as far as comprehension is concerned, and may be more acceptable than mistakes of socio-cultural competence, as far as behavior and effective communication is concerned. *Move Up* attempts to establish grammar and language functions in their pivotal position, but without neglecting the other strands of the multi-syllabus design.

Vocabulary

There are two important criteria for the inclusion of words in the vocabulary boxes. Firstly, they are words which the pre-intermediate learner should acquire in order to communicate successfully in a number of social or transactional situations. Secondly, they may also be words which are generated by the reading or listening material, and are considered suitable for the pre-intermediate level. However, an overriding principle operates: there is usually an activity which allows learners to focus on and, one hopes, acquire the words which are personally relevant to them. This involves a process of personal selection or grouping of words according to personal categories. It is hard to acquire words which one doesn't need, so this approach responds to the learner's individual requirements and personal motivation. *Move Up* Pre-intermediate presents approximately 950 words in the vocabulary boxes for the learner's active attention, but each learner must decide which words to focus on. The *Wordbank* in the Practice Book encourages students to store the words they need in categories which are relevant to them.

Reading

The reading passages are generally at a higher level than one might expect for learners at pre-intermediate level. Foreign language users who are not of near-native speaker competence are constantly confronted with difficult language, and to expose the learners to examples of real-life English in the reassuring context of the classroom is to help prepare them for the conditions of real life. There is always an activity or two which encourages the learner to respond to the passage either on a personal level or to focus on its main ideas. *Move Up* attempts to avoid a purely pedagogical approach to reading, and encourages the learner to respond to the reading passage in a personal and genuine way before using it for other purposes.

Listening

Listening is based on a similar approach to reading in *Move Up*. Learners are often exposed to examples of natural, authentic English in order to prepare them for real-life situations in which they will have to listen to ungraded English. But the tasks are always graded for the learners' particular level. Learners at pre-intermediate level are often pleased by how much they understand. Learners at higher levels are often disappointed by how little they understand. A number of different native and non-native accents are used in the listening passages to reflect the fact that in real life very few speakers using English speak with standard American or British pronunciation.

Speaking

Many opportunities are given for speaking, particularly in pairwork and groupwork. Learners are encouraged to work in pairs and groups because the number of learners in most classes does not allow the teacher to give undivided attention to each learner's English. In these circumstances, it is important for the teacher to evaluate whether fluency or accuracy is the most important criterion. On most occasions in *Move Up* Pre-intermediate, speaking practice in the *Grammar* sections is concerned with accuracy, and in the *Speaking* sections with fluency. In the latter sections, it is better not to interrupt and correct the learners until after the activity has finished.

Writing

The writing activities in *Move Up* are based on guided paragraph writing with work on making notes, turning notes into sentences, and joining sentences into paragraphs with various linking devices. The activities are quite tightly controlled. This is not to suggest that more creative work is not valid, but it is one of the responsibilities of a coursebook to provide a systematic grounding in the skill. More creative writing is covered in the Practice Book. Work is also done on punctuation, and most of the writing activities are based on real-life tasks, such as writing letters and cards.

Sounds

Pronunciation, stress, and intonation work tends to interrupt the communicative flow of a lesson, and there is a temptation to leave it out in the interests of maintaining the momentum of an activity sequence. In *Move Up* there is work on sounds in most lessons, usually just before the stage where the learners have to use the new structures orally in pairwork or groupwork. At this level, it seems suitable to introduce work beyond the straightforward system of English phonemes, most of which the learners will be able to reproduce accurately because the same phonemes exist in their own language. So activities which focus on stress in words and sentences, and on the implied meaning of certain intonation patterns, are included. The model for pronunciation is American English.

Topics

The main topics covered in *Move Up* Pre-intermediate include personal identification, house and home, daily life, leisure activities, travel, relations with other people, health, education, shopping, food and drink, geographical location, and the environment. On many occasions, the words presented in the vocabulary box all belong to a particular word field or topic.

Learner Training

Implicit in the overall approach is the development of learner training to encourage learners to take responsibility for their own learning. Examples of this are regular opportunities to use monolingual and bilingual dictionaries, ways of organizing vocabulary according to personal categories, and inductive grammar work.

Cross-cultural Training

Much of the material and activities in *Move Up* creates the opportunity for cross-cultural training. Most learners will be using English as a medium of communication with other non-native speakers, and certainly with people of different cultures. Errors of socio-cultural competence are likely to be less easily tolerated than errors of grammar or lexical insufficiency. But it is impossible to give the learners enough specific information about a culture because it is impossible to predict all the cultural circumstances in which they will use their newly acquired language competence. Information about *sample* cultures, such as the United States and Britain, as well as non-English speaking ones, is given to allow the learners to compare their own culture with another. This creates opportunities for learners to reflect on their own culture in order to become more aware of the possibility of different attitudes, behavior, customs, traditions, and beliefs in other cultures. In this spirit, cross-cultural training is possible even with groups where the learners all come from the same cultural background. There are interesting and revealing differences between people from the same region or town, or even between friends and members of the same family. Exploring these will help the learners become not merely proficient in the language, but competent in the overall aim of communication.

Level and Progress

One important principle behind *Move Up* is that the learners arrive at pre-intermediate level with very different language abilities and requirements. Some may find the early lessons very easy and will be able to move quickly on to later lessons. The way *Move Up* is structured, with individual lessons of approximately 90 minutes, means that these learners can confirm that they have acquired a certain area of grammar, language function, and vocabulary, consolidate this competence with activities giving practice in the other aspects of the course design, and then move on. Others may find that their previous language competence needs to be reactivated more carefully and slowly. The core teaching lesson in the Student's Book may not provide them with enough practice material to ensure that the given grammar, language functions, and vocabulary have been firmly acquired. For these learners, extra practice may be needed and is provided in both the Practice Book (for self-study work) and by the Resource Packs (for classroom work). If learners return to language training at pre-intermediate level after a long period of little or no practice, it is hard to predict what they still know. *Move Up* is designed to help this kind of learner as much as those who need to confirm that they have already acquired a basic knowledge of English.

Correction

You may need to tell your students your policy on correction. Some may expect you to correct every mistake; others will be hesitant to join in if they are nervous about correction. You need to decide when, and how often you want to correct people. Of course, this will depend on the person and the activity, but it might be worth making the distinction between activities which encourage accuracy, in which it is very suitable to provide a certain amount of correction, and activities which focus on fluency, in which it may be better to note down mistakes and give them to the student at a later stage. Another approach may be to encourage accuracy at the beginning of a practice sequence and fluency towards the end. Let them know the general principles. It will create a positive impression even for those who may, at first, disagree with it.

Interest and Motivation

Another important principle in the course design has been the intrinsic interest of the materials. Interesting material motivates the learners, and motivated learners acquire the language more effectively. The topics have been carefully selected so that they are interesting to adults and young adults, with a focus on areas which would engage their general leisure-time interests. This is designed to generate what might be described as authentic motivation, the kind of motivation we have when we read a newspaper or watch a television program. But it is obvious that we cannot motivate all learners all of the time. They may arrive at a potentially motivating lesson with little desire to learn on this particular occasion, perhaps for reasons that have nothing to do with the teacher, the course, or the material. It is therefore necessary to introduce tasks which attract what might be described as pedagogic or artificial motivation, tasks which would not usually be performed in real life, but which engage the learner in an artificial, but no less effective way.

Variety of Material and Language

Despite the enormous amount of research done on language acquisition, no one has come up with a definitive description of how we acquire either our native language or a foreign language which takes account of every language learner or the teaching style of every teacher. Every learner has different interests and different requirements, and every teacher has a different style and approach to what they teach. *Move Up* attempts to adopt an approach which appeals to differing styles of learning and teaching. The pivotal role of grammar and vocabulary is reflected in the material, but not at the expense of the development of the skills or pronunciation. An integrated multi-syllabus course design, designed to respond to the broad variety of learners' requirements and teachers' objectives, is at the heart of *Move Up's* approach.

RESEARCH

Heinemann ELT is committed to continuing research into coursebook development. Many teachers contributed to the evolution of *Move Up* through piloting and reports, and we now want to continue this process of feedback by inviting users of *Move Up*— both teachers and students—to tell us about their experience of working with the course. If you or your colleagues have any comments, questions or suggestions, please address them to the Publisher, Adult Group, Heinemann ELT, Halley Court, Jordan Hill, Oxford OX2 8EJ or contact your local Heinemann representative.

Map of the Book

Lesson	Grammar and functions	Vocabulary	Skills and sounds
1 *How Are You Doing?* Your body and your health	Present perfect simple (1) for experiences	Parts of the body	**Reading:** reading and answering a questionnaire **Speaking:** talking about experiences
2 *What's New With You?* Talking about changes in your life	Present perfect simple (2) for past actions with present results.	Feelings	**Listening:** listening for specific information **Sounds:** linking of /v/ and /s/ endings before certain verbs **Writing:** writing a letter describing recent changes in your life
3 *It's a Holiday!* Important national or local events and festivals	Present perfect simple (3): *for* and *since*	Words to describe important events and festivals	**Listening:** listening for specific information **Sounds:** weak form /ə/ **Writing:** writing a paragraph describing an important national occasion
4 *Divided by a Common Language* A comparison of American and British English	Restrictive relative clauses: *who*, *which/that*, and *where*	American English words with different meanings in British English	**Speaking:** talking about useful types of English **Reading:** inferring **Sounds:** comparing American and British standard pronunciation; differences in specific phonemes **Listening:** listening for specific information
5 *What's It Called in English?* Describing objects	Describing things when you don't know the word	Adjectives for shape, material, size, etc. Words to describe something if you don't know the English word Everyday objects	**Listening:** listening for main ideas **Sounds:** consonant clusters; word linking in sentences **Speaking:** describing everyday objects
Fluency 1 *Strangers and Friends* **Small talk**			
Progress Check Lessons 1–5	Review	Verbs from nouns and nouns from verbs Noun suffixes Meanings of *get*	**Sounds:** /ɜ:/ and /ə/; /ɒ/ and /ʌ/ **Speaking:** talking about your travel experiences **Writing:** writing a paragraph about other students' travel experiences
6 *Driver's Ed* Instructions and rules for driving	*Have to* and *have got to* for obligation	Words to describe situations where instructions apply; on a freeway, at the airport, in a bar, on a bus	**Speaking:** talking about safety instructions **Sounds:** linking of /gɒtə/ and /hæftə/ **Reading:** reading about driving instructions **Listening:** listening for main ideas
7 *The Skylight* A short story by Penelope Mortimer	Modal verbs *Can, could* (1) for ability	New words from a story *The Skylight*	**Speaking:** talking about what you can or can't do; predicting what happens next in a story **Listening:** listening for main ideas; listening for specific information
8 *Breaking the Rules?* Rules and customs in everyday situations in different countries	*Can, can't* (2) for permission and prohibition	Words to describe rules in everyday situations	**Reading:** reading and answering a questionnaire **Sounds:** strong and weak forms of *can* **Listening:** listening for main ideas **Speaking:** talking about rules
9 *Warning: Flying Is Bad For Your Health* Advice on staying healthy	*Should* and *shouldn't* for advice	Medical complaints Parts of the body	**Reading:** reading for specific information **Listening:** listening for specific information **Speaking:** talking about advice for staying healthy
10 *Doing Things the Right Way* Behavior and manners in different social situations	Asking for permission Asking people to do things Offering	Words from a questionnaire about behavior in social situations	**Reading:** reading and answering a questionnaire **Sounds:** polite intonation in questions **Listening:** listening for specific information
Fluency 2 *How Do You Feel?* **Expressing feelings; reacting**			
Progress Check Lessons 6–10	Review	Adjectives and nouns which go together Words with more than one meaning and part of speech Techniques for dealing with words you don't understand Word association	**Sounds:** /əʊ/ and /ɔɪ/; /ʃ/, /tʃ/ and /dʒ/; polite and friendly intonation **Speaking:** talking about advice and rules for foreign visitors to your country **Writing:** writing some advice and rules for foreign visitors

Lesson	Grammar and functions	Vocabulary	Skills and sounds
11 *The Stranger* An excerpt from *The Bridges of Madison County* by Robert James Waller	Past continuous (1) for interrupted actions: *when*	New words from an excerpt from *The Bridges of Madison County*	**Speaking:** predicting what happens next in a story **Listening:** listening for specific information **Writing:** writing a story
12 *A Walk Through Time* A true story about a woman who traveled back in time	Past continuous (2): *while* and *when*	New words from a passage called *A Walk Through Time*	**Reading:** predicting; reading for main ideas **Speaking:** talking about traveling in time
13 *Is There a Future For Us?* Two children give their views on the environment in the future	Expressions of quantity: *too much/many, not enough, fewer, less,* and *more*	Geographical features and location	**Reading:** reading for specific information; inferring **Speaking:** talking about the geography of your country; talking about the environment
14 *The Day of the Dead* An article about Mexico's Day of the Dead	Present simple passive	Rituals and festivals	**Reading:** predicting; reading for main ideas; reacting to a passage **Speaking:** talking about a ritual or festival in your country **Writing:** writing about a ritual or festival
15 *Table Manners* Table manners and behaviour in social situations	Making comparisons: *but, although, however*	Food Plates, cutlery, etc. Cooking utensils	**Reading:** reading and answering a questionnaire **Listening:** listening for specific information **Sounds:** stress and intonation in sentences with *but, however, although* **Speaking:** talking and writing about table manners and social occasions in your country
Fluency 3 *Women and Men* **Expressing opinions**			
Progress Check Lessons 11–15	Review	Multi-part verbs	**Sounds:** /f/ and /p/; /h/; stress in multi-part verbs **Writing:** punctuating a story; inserting words into a story
16 *Hot Enough For You?* The best times to visit different countries	*May* and *might* for possibility	Weather	**Reading:** reading for specific information **Writing:** writing a letter giving advice about the best time to visit your country
17 *Help!* Emergency situations	First conditional	Words to describe emergency situations	**Speaking:** talking about emergency situations; predicting the end of a story **Sounds:** word linking in sentences **Listening:** listening for main ideas, listening for specific information
18 *My Perfect Weekend* A woman describes her perfect weekend	*Would* for imaginary situations	Luxuries and necessities New vocabulary from a passage called *My Perfect Weekend*	**Speaking:** talking about luxuries and necessities; talking about your perfect weekend **Reading:** reacting to a passage **Sounds:** linking of /d/ ending before verbs beginning in /t/ or /d/ **Listening:** listening for main ideas
19 *The Umbrella Man* A short story by Roald Dahl	Second conditional	New vocabulary from a story called *The Umbrella Man*	**Reading:** predicting; reading for main ideas; reading for specific information **Listening:** listening for specific information **Writing:** rewriting a story from a different point of view
20 *The Wonderful Pearl* A folk tale from Vietnam	Past perfect	New vocabulary from a story called *The Wonderful Pearl*	**Listening:** listening for specific information **Sounds:** linking of /d/ in past perfect sentences **Speaking:** predicting the end of a story **Writing:** writing a folk tale from your country
Fluency 4 *Dos and Don'ts* **Giving advice**			
Progress Check Lessons 16 – 20	Review	*Make* and *do* Formation of adverbs	**Sounds:** /w/, /r/; /ɔ:/, /aʊ/; stressed words **Speaking:** talking about difficult situations; preparing and acting out a dialogue

1

GENERAL COMMENTS

Present perfect simple (1)

This is the first of three lessons on the present perfect simple. This lesson concentrates on how the tense can be used to describe experiences. The key concept with this use is that we are not interested in when the action in the past was performed. As soon as we need to use an expression of past time, the past simple is required instead of the present perfect. The tense is a difficult one for students to master. They have to learn to manipulate the form, which involves past participles, and the concept. Some languages may have a tense which looks like the present perfect but which operates like the past simple.

How Are You Doing?

The theme of the lesson focuses on two important vocabulary fields, parts of the body and illness. While the students may need this vocabulary one day in serious circumstances, the context here is intended to be lighthearted.

Cross-cultural awareness

Most Americans use the questions *How are you?* and *How are you doing?* as a greeting or a way of starting a conversation. It is not intended as a serious enquiry about someone's health, and should not be perceived as being unacceptably curious or personal. Ask your students if their native language has a similar greeting.

READING

1. Aim: to prepare for reading.

● Ask the students to think about their health, and about staying fit. Ask different people what they do to stay fit, if anything. You may like to ask them to suggest ways of staying in good shape and make a list of these suggestions on the board.

2. Aim: to read and react to a questionnaire.

● Questionnaires establish an immediate relationship with the reader, and their reactions to it constitute the reading comprehension check. Ask the students to read and think about their answers to the questions.

● The students may feel ready to share their answers to the questions, but it is better for them to do the next stage in this activity sequence first in order to be sure that they have suitable language to continue.

VOCABULARY

1. Aim: to present the words in the vocabulary box.

● The students may already know many of these basic items of vocabulary. The items which are already in position on the chart are likely to be the most common. The items which are listed, and should be added to the diagram, are the words which the students need to acquire. Begin the activity by pointing to different parts of your body and asking what they are in English.

● Then ask the students to complete the chart with the words. If possible, it would be better to draw a stick person on the board, and ask students to come up and name each part of the body. Ask them to help each other with identifying the parts of the body.

> **Answers**
> 1. toe 2. knee 3. neck 4. back 5. elbow
> 6. shoulder 7. waist 8. foot 9. thumb
> 10. wrist 11. finger 12. ankle 13. tooth
> 14. mouth 15. eye 16. throat

2. Aim: to find out the names of other parts of the body.

● Ask the students to name the other parts of the body. You can help them by giving them the words on the board, or by suggesting they look the words up in bilingual dictionaries. But of course, it is much better if they can name the parts of the body without help.

3. Aim: to consolidate the acquisition of words to describe parts for the body.

● As a final activity in this sequence, ask the students to write down the words under the four headings.

> **Answers**
> **head:** tooth, mouth, eye, throat, neck, nose, face, ear
> **body:** shoulder, waist, back
> **arm:** finger, wrist, thumb, elbow
> **leg:** knee, ankle, toe, foot

GRAMMAR

1. Aim: to focus on the difference between the present perfect and the past simple.
- Ask the students to read the information about the present perfect simple in the grammar box.

- If necessary, stress the fact that when we use the present perfect to describe experiences, we are not interested in when the experience happened. Ask the students to do the activity.

> **Answers**
> 1. **Have** you ever **been** in an ambulance?
> 2. When **was** the last time you **were** sick?
> 3. **Have** you ever **eaten** *sushi?*
> 4. **Have** you ever **met** a famous person?
> 5. **Have** you ever **played** tennis?
> 6. What **did** you **have** for dinner last night?

2. Aim: to focus on past participles.
- This activity is designed to draw the students' attention to the fact that past participles are used in the formation of the present perfect. This may be a new concept for them. You may like to explain that many past participles are like the past simple form of the verb, and the exceptions are with certain irregular verbs.

> **Answers**
> been, had, said, eaten, played, taught, visited, lived, seen, worked, loved, known, paid, broken, met, made, tried, won, worn, sold

- Write the answers on the board and circle the irregular past participles.

3. Aim: to practice using the present perfect to talk about experiences.
- Ask the students to work in pairs and to talk about their answers to the questionnaire. You may like to check one or two students' answers first. Make sure everyone forms the present perfect with a suitable past participle.

SPEAKING

1. Aim: to practice using the present perfect to talk about experiences.
- The focus of this activity has moved away from parts of the body and personal experiences, and towards more general experiences. Encourage the students to talk about experiences using not only the verbs in *Grammar* activity 2 but also any other suitable verbs. Give them plenty of time to write their questions.

2. Aim: to practice using the present perfect to talk about experiences.
- Ask the students to go around asking and answering their questions about experiences.

- You may like to ask the students to write about other people's experiences for homework.

- At this stage of the lesson, you may find that the students are beginning to manipulate the structure accurately, but without being confident that they will do so on every occasion in the future. You may need to supplement their work with some material from *Move Up* Practice Book or Resource Packs.

2

GENERAL COMMENTS

Present perfect simple (2)

This is the second of three lessons on the present perfect simple tense. This lesson deals with the use of the present perfect to talk about past actions with present results. Although this is a very common use of the present perfect in British English, it is much less common in American English.

Diane's Diary

Diane and her family are fictional characters, but the events described in her diary are by no means unusual occurrences in the United States. By one estimate, two in every ten preschool children are being taken care of by their fathers while their mothers go out to work. This may provide some interesting topics for discussion, especially for students who come from more traditional cultures.

Vocabulary

The vocabulary load in this lesson is not heavy, but there are several "passive" (or -*ed*) adjectives which have parallel "active" (or -*ing*) forms. In general, the -*ed* adjective is used to describe the reaction to a stimulus, while the -*ing* adjectives describe the stimulus itself. For example, we can say "I am interest**ed** (reaction) in politics (stimulus)" or "Politics (stimulus) is very interest**ing**." This is a source of confusion for students whose native language has only one adjective to express both meanings. These pairs of adjectives are very common, however, and it is worth taking the time to explain the difference at this point.

VOCABULARY AND READING

1. **Aim: to present the vocabulary in the box; to distinguish between parts of speech.**
● Ask the students to look at the words in the box and decide which are adjectives and which are verbs in the infinitive.

> **Answers**
> afford *v* bored *adj* celebrate *v* close *v* and *adj*
> complain *v* depressed *adj* excited *adj*
> exhausted *adj* jealous *adj* promote *v*
> qualified *adj* scream *v* become *v* foreign *adj*

2. **Aim: to predict what the reading is going to be about; to prepare for reading.**
● Tell the students that they are going to read extracts from the diary of Diane, a homemaker who lives in Oklahoma City. Ask them to imagine what her life is like, and then to predict which of the words in the vocabulary box are likely to appear in her diary. Encourage the students to say why they would expect to see the words that they choose.

3. **Aim: to read and infer.**
● Tell the students not to worry about the spaces for dates under each extract for the moment. Ask them to work in pairs and try to put the extracts in order. Tell them there is more than one possible order, but that some extracts must logically follow others.

LISTENING

1. **Aim: to listen for main ideas; to check answers.**
● Tell the students that the extracts that Diane reads include more information than those in the Student's Book, so they will have to listen very carefully to find the correct order.

● 📼 Play the tape and tell students to check their answers to *Vocabulary and Reading* activity 3

2. **Aim: to listen for specific information.**
● 📼 Play the tape again and ask the students to write down the date of each extract.

> **Answers**
> [7] I've just been promoted. This means more pay—but also longer hours.
>   Date: **October 28, 1996**
> [3] Ben has just turned two. We celebrated his birthday with pizza and a chocolate cake, but we couldn't really afford any nice presents.
>   Date: **January 22, 1996**
> [6] Chuck and Ben have become so close—I think I'm a little bit jealous of Chuck, but I'm really enjoying my job. And I really think Chuck likes being at home now.
>   Date: **July 4, 1996**
> [4] I've found a job! I'm going to work as a saleswoman in a department store. Chuck is going to stay home and take care of Ben, but he's not too happy about it… He thinks he's going to be bored!
>   Date: **February 14, 1996**
> [2] What a sad Christmas. Chuck is really depressed. He's tried so hard to find another job, but he's had no luck.
>   Date: **December 27, 1995**
> [8] I can't believe it… Ben is going to be three tomorrow! We've bought him a great train set—but I think Chuck is more excited to play with it than Ben!
>   Date: **January 21, 1997**
> [1] Chuck has lost his job at the car factory. They're going to close the factory because they've decided to move it to a foreign country. What are we going to do?
>   Date: **October 10, 1995**
> [5] I've just finished my first day at work. I'm exhausted, Ben is screaming, and Chuck is complaining that he has too much housework to do—and he hasn't even made dinner yet!
>   Date: **February 19, 1996**

3.
Aim: to check comprehension of the story; to focus on use of present continuous.

● Ask the students to match the pairs of sentences from Diane's diary without looking at the extracts in their books. Tell them that sentences a–f are the results of sentences 1–6.

4.
Aim: to check answers.

● ▢ Play the tape again and ask the students to check their answers to activity 3. Ask them if they heard any new information about Diane and her family.

> **Answers**
>
> 1. c   2. e   3. f   4. b   5. a   6. d

GRAMMAR

1.
Aim: to focus on the formation of past participles.

● Ask the students to read the information about the present perfect simple in the grammar box.

● Ask them to do the activity. They will have done some work in Lesson 1 on the formation of past participles.

> **Answers**
>
> | | | |
> |---|---|---|
> | lose | lost | lost* |
> | finish | finished | finished* |
> | decide | decided | decided* |
> | buy | bought | bought* |
> | try | tried | tried* |
> | make | made | made* |
> | become | became | become |
> | find | found | found* |
> | write | wrote | written |
> | read | read | read* |
> | drink | drank | drunk |
>
> The verbs marked * have the same form in the past simple and the past participle.

2.
Aim: to practice forming the present perfect.

● Ask the students to do the activity. Explain that the word *now* indicates a change in the life of the person mentioned in each sentence, and suggests a present perfect in the preceding clause.

> **Answers**
>
> 1. I've **bought** a new car, and now I drive to work.
> 2. He's **moved** house, and now he lives in San Francisco.
> 3. She's **finished** her book and is now watching TV.
> 4. We've **drunk** the whole bottle. It's empty.
> 5. I've **found** my bag. It's here.
> 6. She's **written** me a letter, and I'm reading it now.

SOUNDS

Aim: to focus on the sound of the auxiliary *'ve* and *'s* in the present perfect.

● ▢ Play the tape and pause after the first pair of sentences. Ask the students if they noticed how similar they sounded. Point out that you don't always hear *'ve* and *'s*. Repeat with the second pair of sentences, etc.

● ▢ Remind the students that the context will help them decide if the verb is present perfect or past simple. Play the tape and ask them to repeat the sentences.

SPEAKING AND WRITING

1.
Aim: to talk about life today and life a year ago; to prepare for the distinction between the present perfect and the past simple.

● This activity is important in establishing the conceptual framework for showing the difference between the present perfect and the past simple. Make a list on the board of things in your life which are different today. Think about your teaching circumstances and, if appropriate, your personal life, too. There may have been some major changes in government, politics, etc. Try to write at least four or five points on the board to show what you expect of the students.

● Ask the students to do the same with notes about their own lives.

2.
Aim: to talk about changes in your life; to practice speaking.

● Tell the students to look at their notes from activity 1 and think of three sentences which describe the changes that have taken place. Tell them to think of an additional sentence which talks about a change that has actually not taken place.

● When the students have finished preparing their sentences, ask them to work in pairs and tell their partners the four changes.

3.
Aim: to practice speaking; to distinguish between present perfect and past simple.

● Encourage the students to ask questions in order to discover which of their partner's sentences was false. Remind them that statements and questions about specific times (including questions with *when*) must be in the past simple.

4.
Aim: to prepare for writing.

● The purpose of this activity is to generate ideas for the writing activity that follows, so encourage the students to use their imaginations in thinking about what changes they would make if they won the lottery.

5.
Aim: to write an informal letter.

● Ask the students to write a letter using their ideas from activity 4, beginning as shown in the model.

● If time is short, you can ask the students to do this activity for homework.

3

GENERAL COMMENTS

Present perfect simple (3)

This is the third lesson in a series of three which focus on the use of the present perfect simple. By now, the students may be forming the tense accurately and using it with some degree of fluency. This lesson deals with the common use of the present perfect with *for* and *since* and focuses on verbs that are not usually used in the continuous form. Other uses of the present perfect, notably with *yet* and *already*, and the present perfect continuous will be covered in *Move Up* Intermediate.

VOCABULARY AND LISTENING

1. Aim: to introduce the theme of the lesson.

● Ask the students to work in pairs and make a list of important events or festivals in their country. Suggest they choose national rather than religious occasions, as the latter will be covered in Lesson 14. You may like to do this activity orally with the whole class; if so, write the names of the important occasions on the board. Try to leave these names on the board as they will be useful for *Grammar* activity 2.

2. Aim: to present the words in the vocabulary box; to pre-teach some important vocabulary in the listening passage.

● Ask the students to choose the words they can use to describe what happens during the important occasions you have listed in activity 1.

● In the *Writing* section, they will be asked to write about an important event or festival, so use this opportunity to supply them with the necessary vocabulary. You can group the new items under the names of the occasions on the board.

3. Aim: to listen for specific information.

● This is a jigsaw listening activity. Divide the class into two groups, A and B, and ask each group to follow its instructions in the relevant Communication Activity.

● ▭ Play the tape.

● Allow enough time for every member of each group to find out the same information, which they should write down.

4. Aim: to exchange information; to complete the chart.

● Ask the students to work with someone from another group and to exchange information to complete the chart. They are only allowed to reveal the information they have written down in activity 3.

Answers	
What's it called?	The Melbourne Cup.
When does it take place?	The first Tuesday in November at 2:40 P.M.
Where does it take place?	Flemington race course, Melbourne, Australia.
When did it first take place?	1874.
What happens?	People from all over Australia come to Melbourne for the day with picnics, and they bet on the horse they think will win.
Is it a public holiday?	Only in the city of Melbourne and the State of Victoria.
Are there any other interesting features?	Everyone in Australia stops work to listen.

5. Aim: to listen for specific information.

● ▭ Play the tape again, so the students can check their answers.

● When they're ready, they can work in pairs and see if they can add any extra information. Check this stage with the whole class.

6. Aim: to practice talking about important events and festivals.

● The chart, and possibly the answers, will give the students the necessary framework and language to talk about an important day in their country. This is an important stage in the preparation for writing later in the lesson.

GRAMMAR

1. Aim: to focus on the difference between *for* and *since*.

● Ask the students to read the information about the present perfect simple in the grammar box.

● Ask the students to complete the sentences.

> **Answers**
> 1. They've had a parade **since** 1988.
> 2. There have been fireworks **for** ten years.
> 3. It's been a national holiday **since** 1993.
> 4. The president has given a speech every year **for** five years.
> 5. She's been Queen **since** March.
> 6. We've celebrated Independence Day **for** ten years.

2. Aim: to practice using the present perfect with *for* and *since*.

● Ask students to say how long their countries have celebrated the important occasions they noted down in *Vocabulary and Listening* activity 1. These occasions may still be on the board for you to point to. Ask them to make statements using *for* and *since*.

SOUNDS

Aim: to focus on the weak form pronunciation of *for*.

● 🔊 Draw the students' attention to the weak form pronunciation of *for*. Play the tape and ask them to repeat the sentences. Pause after each sentence.

WRITING

1. Aim: to provide a purpose for reading the model writing passage.

● Ask the students to read about Thanksgiving and to answer the questions. The passage is going to be used as a model for guided writing in activity 2.

> **Answers**
> a. Since 1789.
> b. The first harvest of the Pilgrims.
> c. Families get together, prepare and eat a big meal, and then watch football on TV.
> d. Turkey, sweet potatoes, squash, cranberries, and pumpkins.

2. Aim: to use the model passage to write a passage about another important national occasion.

● Ask the students to write about their own important event or festival.

● If time is short, they may like to do this activity for homework.

4

GENERAL COMMENTS

American and British English

This lesson covers some of the main differences between American English and British English. Inevitably, it is a fairly brief overview and will leave out more than it can include. However, it is important to stress that the main differences are to do with vocabulary. American English and British English accents are mutually intelligible, and the differences in spelling and grammar usually present few problems of comprehension. The lesson focuses on some of these vocabulary differences, and makes the student aware that other differences may exist. It should be added that the context can usually resolve any confusion which may arise.

SPEAKING AND READING

1. Aim: to practice talking about attitudes towards American and British English; to prepare for reading.
  • Many students have a natural preference towards American or British English. This activity encourages the students to confront their preference towards and their prejudice against American or British English. There is, of course, no right or wrong answer. Encourage your students to explain why they prefer one or the other. It may be better to do this activity orally with the whole class.

2. Aim: to read and infer.
  • Ask the students to read the statements and then read the passage to find out if the statements are true or false. The answer is not always obvious; students may have to infer what the writer means.

Answers
1. False 2. True 3. True 4. True

GRAMMAR

1. Aim: to focus on restrictive relative clauses.
  • Ask the students to read the information about restrictive relative clauses in the grammar box.

  • Ask the students to do the activity.

Answers
  1. A hat is something **which/that** you wear on your head.
  2. A post office is a place **where** you can buy stamps and mail letters.
  3. A journalist is someone **who** writes for a newspaper.
  4. A swimsuit is something **which/that** you wear when you go swimming.
  5. A disco is a place **where** you go to dance.
  6. A hairbrush is something **which/that** you use to brush your hair.

2. Aim: to practice writing restrictive relative clauses.
  • Do the activity orally, and help the students with any necessary vocabulary.

Possible Answers
A kitchen is a place where you cook food.
A supermarket is a place where you can buy food.
A language teacher is someone who teaches a language.
A refrigerator is a place where you keep food and drink cold.
A pilot is someone who flies a plane.
Shoes are something that you wear on your feet.
A restaurant is a place where you can have lunch or dinner.
A bar is a place where you can have a drink and meet friends.

  • Ask the students to write the definitions.

  • There is more work on restrictive relative clauses with objects in Lesson 5.

SOUNDS

1. **Aim: to compare American and British pronunciation.**

● 🔲 Many students can recognize an American or a British accent, but are not aware why they sound different. This activity gives students an opportunity to compare the two with each other. Play the tape and ask the students to listen to an American speaker and then to a British speaker.

● 🔲 Ask the students to listen and guess if the speaker is American or British. Play the tape.

Answer
The speaker is an American.

2. **Aim: to present the basic differences of British and American pronunciation.**

● 🔲 This activity can only cover some of the main differences between standard American and standard British pronunciation. Regional accents may vary even more. Simply play the tape and ask students to listen. If they want to repeat the words in a British, then an American way, they can, but you need to agree with them which accent they wish to model their own accent on.

VOCABULARY AND LISTENING

1. **Aim: to present the American and British words in the vocabulary boxes.**

● Whether the students choose to acquire American or British English, it is still useful, at least for receptive purposes, to be aware of some words which may cause confusion. The words in the boxes are the words featured in the reading passage.

Answers

American English	British English
chips	crisps
crosswalk	zebra crossing
drugstore	chemist's
french fries	chips
main street	high street
pants	trousers
public school	state school
subway	underground

2. **Aim: to check the answers to activity 1, and to listen for specific information.**

● 🔲 Ask the students to listen and check their answers to activity 1.

5

GENERAL COMMENTS

What's It Called in English?

The theme of this lesson is how to make yourself understood if you don't know the word for something; a survival skill for circumstances with which your students may be very familiar. An ability to describe something's purpose or appearance in the absence of the word for the thing itself will greatly contribute to the student's fluency. Students may have difficulty with prepositions coming at the end of a sentence, e.g. *It's something to write on.* *It's for drinking wine out of* because it is a construction which doesn't often occur in other languages.

Accents

The speakers in the listening passage are all non-native speakers and speak with characteristic accents. Students are more likely to hear English spoken by non-native speakers of the language than by native speakers, and certainly by speakers of standard American English. It is important, therefore, that students are exposed to as many different accents as possible. However, please note that the accents in this lesson are not proposed as models for pronunciation.

VOCABULARY AND SPEAKING

1. Aim: to present the words in the vocabulary box.
- Write the words for four or five very simple objects on the board, e.g. *table, book, pen, tire, curtains.* Ask the students to look at the words in the box and to suggest words they could use to describe the objects.

- Ask the students to choose five or six words in the box and think of things they can describe with each one.

2. Aim: to categorize the words in the vocabulary box.
- The process of categorizing the words will reinforce the learning process.

> **Answers**
> **What does it feel like?** hard, heavy, light, soft
> **What's it made of?** cloth, cotton, glass, leather, metal, nylon, paper, plastic, rubber, stone, wood, wool
> **What shape is it?** curved, oblong, oval, round, square
> **What size is it?** high, long, low, narrow, short, wide

3. Aim: to present the words in the vocabulary box.
- The words are particularly useful when you're describing the function of something.

> **Possible Answers**
> **liquid:** water, oil
> **machine:** dishwasher, lawnmower
> **powder:** laundry detergent, soap powder
> **stuff:** toothpaste, lipstick, shampoo
> **thing:** stove, television
> **tool:** hammer, spoon

- Explain that a machine is something that works on its own, and does something a human can do. For example, you wouldn't call a *television* a machine.

4. Aim: to present all the words in the vocabulary box.
- Ask the students to match the words with the items in the pictures.

LISTENING

1. Aim: to prepare for listening.
- Ask the students to look at the objects in the pictures and to find words in the vocabulary boxes to describe them. You may want to write the words for the objects on the board and ask the students to suggest suitable words.

2. Aim: to listen for main ideas.
- 🔲 The speakers in the listening passages don't know the word for one of the objects in the pictures. This can happen even to advanced speakers of English. This is a productive comprehension check in that the students have to produce language to demonstrate comprehension, but they only have to write a single word each time; alternatively, you can do the task orally. You can also stop the tape after each description to allow the students plenty of time.

> **Answers**
> 1. glue
> 2. towel
> 3. matches
> 4. sunscreen
> 5. vacuum cleaner

3. Aim: to present the target language.
- Each description shows an example of the different constructions used for describing things when you don't know the word.

> **Answers**
> a. sweater b. shoe polish c. blow dryer
> d. camera e. window cleaner f. bag
> g. wine glass h. pad of paper

FUNCTIONS

1. Aim: to focus on the prepositions at the end of the sentence, and on restrictive relative clauses.

● Remind the students, if necessary, that they learned about restrictive relative clauses in Lesson 4. Ask them to read the information in the functions box about describing something when you don't know the word.

● Ask the students to do the activity.

Answers
1. A chair is a thing to sit **on.**
2. A mug is for drinking **out of.**
3. A skillet is for cooking things **in.**
4. A towel is for drying yourself **with.**
5. An oven is for cooking things **in.**
6. A plant pot is a thing for putting plants **in.**

2. Aim: to practice describing things.

● You may like to do this orally, since the students may need help with suitable vocabulary.

Possible Answers
A wallet is oblong, made of leather, and is for keeping money in.
String is long and thin and you use it to tie things up with.
Soap is stuff for washing yourself with.
A can opener is a thing for opening cans.
A sponge is square and soft, and you use it to wash yourself with.

● When the students have done the activity orally, ask them to write down the definitions.

3. Aim: to practice describing things.

● If the preceding activities have been done successfully, ask the students to describe the purpose of the things mentioned on their own.

Answers
1. A sleeping bag is for sleeping in.
2. An envelope is a thing for putting letters in.
3. Laundry detergent is stuff for washing the clothes in a washing machine.
4. A dishwasher is a machine for washing the dishes.
5. A refrigerator is a thing for keeping food and drink cold in.
6. A pen is a tool for writing with.

SOUNDS

1. Aim: to focus on consonant clusters.

● Some students find it difficult to pronounce two or more consonants in a cluster. Ask them to say the words out loud and to merge the consonant clusters together. Be careful that they do not separate them or put in extra vowels to make them easier to say.

● ⌷ Play the tape and pause after each word. Ask the students to listen and check.

2. Aim: to focus on links between words.

● ⌷ In connected speech many words run into each other. If you have time, write these sentences on the board. Play the tape and pause after each sentence. Ask the students to listen and notice which words run into each other. Mark the links on the board.

Answers

Is it heavy?

An egg is oval.

A refrigerator is cold.

It's for opening cans.

It's something to write on.

To open, pull it out.

SPEAKING

Aim: to practice communication strategies.
● The game is designed to help students practice different ways of making themselves understood. You will need between five and ten minutes to do it.

● First, ask one student from each group to come up to you. Whisper the first item in the list of words below to these students. Make sure the others in the group don't hear.

   1. a sleeping bag 2. an umbrella 3. a suitcase
   4. a shower 5. a traveler's check 6. scissors
   7. a passport 8. lettuce 9. a watch 10. an aspirin

● The players return to their groups and describe, draw, mime, or point to the object. They must not say what it is. When someone guesses correctly, this student comes to you and whispers the word. If it is correct, you tell him or her the next word. You continue until a group has guessed all the words. If time is short, you can leave out some of the words.

Fluency 1

GENERAL COMMENTS

The focus of the socio-cultural training in this Fluency lesson is on relationships between people who do not know each other, such as in customer-service situations. A notable characteristic of Americans is their friendliness towards strangers, but this is often replaced by a certain distance. Non-Americans are often delighted by the warmth an American may show when they first meet, and disappointed when this intimacy disappears on a subsequent occasion. The language used often means less than it might appear to. The common expression *We must have lunch!* or *We must have a drink!* may not be the friendly invitation it appears, and the superficiality of such meaningless exchanges often causes confusion.

Despite this, Americans are famous for being a *low contact culture*, that is to say, one in which people do not touch each other very much. Ask the students to decide if they belong to a *high contact culture* or a *low contact culture*.

Like the superficial invitations, *small talk* is language which means less than it appears, but its function is to oil the wheels of social interaction. The language in the functions box is presented not so much for productive as for receptive use. Encourage the students to think about if there is much small talk in their own culture, and if so, how much.

LISTENING AND SPEAKING

1. Aim: to prepare for listening; to practice understanding text organization.
- Explain the topic of the lesson, and ask students if they ever speak to strangers, and if so, in what circumstances. Find out who responds to or strikes up conversations with strangers in the following situations: *in a train/bus, at a bus stop, in a line, in stores, in waiting rooms.*

- Ask the students to read the conversation and decide where the sentences go.

- Ask the students to check their answers in pairs.

> **Answers**
> 1. a   2. c   3. b   4. d   5. e

- 🔲 Ask the students to listen and check their answers.

2. Aim: to practice speaking.
- Explain that it's always important to analyze the context of a conversation, as there will be many clues to its meaning. In the classroom, the students are often deprived of much of the contextual help they would otherwise receive in real life.

- Ask the students to discuss their answers to the questions.

> **Answers**
> They are at a bus stop or in a subway.
> They are waiting for a bus or a train.

3. Aim: to practice speaking.
- Ask the students to act out the conversation in pairs.

- Ask two or three pairs to act out the conversation to the whole class.

4. Aim: to prepare for listening.
- Ask the students to work alone and think about their answers to the statements. You may like to deal with any difficult vocabulary at this stage.

5. Aim: to prepare for listening; to practice speaking.

● Ask the students to work in pairs and talk about their answers.

● You may like to conduct some group feedback on the statements at this stage.

6. Aim: to practice listening for main ideas.

● 🎞 By now the students should be well prepared for this listening activity. Play the tape and ask the students simply to check the statements which Gary says are true for the United States.

Answers

United States

We never speak to people we don't know.

We always talk to our neighbors even if we don't know them very well.

We never greet people with a kiss.

We often use first names as soon as we meet strangers. ✔

We smile when we're embarrassed or don't want to hurt someone's feelings.

Man stand up when a women enters the room. ✔

Men always let women enter a room first. ✔

We say hello and goodbye to store clerks, even in large stores.

---

7. Aim: to practice speaking; to provide an opportunity for a second listening.

● Ask the students to try to remember the details of what Gary said. Write as many details as they can suggest on the board.

● 🎞 Play the tape again and check the details on the board which are correct.

FUNCTIONS

1. Aim: to compare English with the students' language.

● This activity invites the students to compare English with their own language.

● Ask the students to read the information about small talk in the functions box. Find out if there are any direct translations, or simply expressions which mean more or less the same as the English. You may like to ask the students to do this activity in writing, or orally with the whole class.

2. Aim: to practice using the language in the functions box.

● Ask the students to work in pairs and to discuss what they might say in the situations described.

● Check the students' answers with the whole class.

Possible Answers

You want to attract someone's attention: *Excuse me; Pardon me.*

You leave a store: *Have a nice day!*

Someone thanks you: *You're welcome; That's OK.*

You ask someone for something: *Please.*

Someone says something surprising: *Really?; Is that so?; You don't say!*

You say goodbye to friends before the weekend: *See you (later)!; So long!*

You bump into someone: *Excuse me; I'm sorry.*

You sneeze: *Excuse me; Pardon me.*

You arrive late: *Excuse me; I'm sorry.*

You want to start a conversation with someone: *It's a beautiful day, isn't it?*

You see someone who looks lost: *Can I help you?*

READING AND SPEAKING

1. Aim: to practice reading for main ideas.

● Matching headings to paragraphs requires the students to understand the passage as a whole, so try to avoid questions about specific items of vocabulary at this stage. This activity will help those learners who insist on understanding every single word to become a little more autonomous and more fluent as readers. Ask them to read the text and to match the headings and the paragraphs.

Answers

Paragraph 1: Talking to Strangers

Paragraph 2: Body Language

Paragraph 3: Touching

Paragraph 4: Saying Goodbye

---

2. Aim: to practice reacting to a text; to practice speaking.

● Ask the students to talk about their reactions to the text, and to compare Americans with people from their own culture. Ask them to look for the most surprising, amusing, or shocking piece of information.

3. Aim: to practice writing.

● Ask the students to write four paragraphs about the features mentioned in the headings in *Reading and Speaking* activity 1. They may like to prepare this in groups of two or three and then write the paragraphs for homework.

Progress Check 1–5

GENERAL COMMENTS

You can work through this Progress Check in the order shown, or concentrate on areas which may have caused difficulty in Lessons 1 to 5. You can also let the students choose the activities which they would like to or feel the need to do.

VOCABULARY

1. **Aim: to focus on noun suffixes.**
● Your students may like to use a dictionary for this activity. Mention that words with the suffixes below are likely to be nouns.

> **Answers**
> govern employ elect educate inform read write
>
> government employment election education information reading writing
>
> entertainment refreshment teaching greeting exhibition connection management

2. **Aim: to focus on a few uses of *get*.**
● As the introduction says, *get* is a very common word in English, and it is not possible to cover all of its meanings. Here are some of the meanings which are most suitable at this level.

> **Answers**
> a. 2 b. 5 c. 6 d. 3 e. 7 f. 1 g. 4

3. **Aim: to help organize the students' vocabulary learning.**
● It may be a suitable moment to take a look at your students' *Wordbanks* in their Practice Books to see if they are completing them successfully.

GRAMMAR

1. **Aim: to review past participles.**

> **Answers**
> been, become, broken, brought, come, done, found, gotten, gone, had, learned, lost, put, read, said, sat, slept, taken, thought, understood, written

2. **Aim: to review short answers in the present perfect.**
● Do this activity orally first of all and check that the students answer using *Yes, I have* or *No, I haven't*.

● Ask the students to write their answers to this activity.

3. **Aim: to review asking questions using the present perfect.**

> **Answers**
> 1. Have you found a new job?
> 2. Have you gotten married?
> 3. Have you stopped smoking?
> 4. Have you bought a motorcycle?
> 5. Have you visited Europe?
> 6. Have you written a book?
> 7. Have you traveled around the United States?
> 8. Have you learned to cook?

4. Aim: to review writing sentences using the present perfect.

> **Answers**
> 1. She's found a new job.
> 2. She hasn't gotten married.
> 3. She's stopped smoking.
> 4. She hasn't bought a motorcycle.
> 5. She's visited Europe.
> 6. She hasn't written a book.
> 7. She's traveled around the United States.
> 8. She hasn't learned to cook.

5. Aim: to review the difference between the present perfect and the simple past.

> **Answers**
> 1. I've never **driven** a car in my life.
> 2. I **left** high school in 1989.
> 3. We **haven't met** before. My name's John.
> 4. Where **did** you **buy** your coat?
> 5. What **did** you **pay** for it?
> 6. How long **have** you **been** married?
> 7. Last Sunday I **got up** at eleven.
> 8. **Have** you **seen** the latest Harrison Ford movie?

6. Aim: to review the use of *for* and *since*.
- The students should answer these questions for themselves.

7. Aim: to review saying what you use things to do.

> **Answers**
> 1. You use an umbrella to keep out of the rain.
> 2. You use sunglasses to protect your eyes from the sun.
> 3. You use adhesive tape to stick paper together with.
> 4. You use an overcoat to keep warm.
> 5. You use a saw to cut wood and metal with.
> 6. You use water to wash, cook, and drink.

8. Aim: to review saying what things are for.

> **Answers**
> 1. A garage is for keeping your car in.
> 2. A bath is for washing yourself in.
> 3. A closet is for keeping your clothes in.
> 4. A toothbrush is for cleaning your teeth with.
> 5. A door handle is for opening the door with.
> 6. A corkscrew is for pulling the corks out of bottles with.

SOUNDS

1. Aim: to focus on /ɜː/ and /ə/.
- 🔲 This activity focuses on stressed and unstressed sounds. Ask the students to put the words in two columns, and then play the tape to listen and check.

> **Answers**
> /ɜː/: surfing fireworks learned heard university word
> /ə/: economics envelope chosen

2. Aim: to focus on /ɒ/ and /ʌ/.
- 🔲 /ɒ/ is a difficult sound for non-native speakers to acquire. This activity is to encourage a very simple distinction between /ɒ/ and /ʌ/. Ask the students to listen to the tape and to repeat each word. Play the tape and pause after each word.

- Ask them to put the words in two columns.

> **Answers**
> /ɒ/: hot awful walking bar oblong
> /ʌ/: up summer bus stuff sunny

SPEAKING AND WRITING

1. Aim: to practice speaking about experiences.
- Ask the students to look at the experiences and to think of other experiences. Do this activity orally with the whole class, and write the activities the students suggest on the board.

2. Aim: to practice speaking about experiences.
- Ask the students to go around the class finding people who have done the things in activity 1. Ask the students to ask for extra information, using the past simple.

3. Aim: to practice writing about experiences.
- The students may like to do this activity for homework.

6

GENERAL COMMENTS

Have to and *have got to*

These two structures are very commonly used to talk about obligation, with *have to* being slightly more formal than *have got to*. The structures operate in exactly the same way as *have* and *have got* (see Book A, Lesson 10) with *have to* being much more common in the question and negative forms. The meaning of *don't have to* may be a source of confusion for some students that have a parallel structure in their own language. The meaning in English is "it is not necessary," in other words it indicates a lack of obligation, whereas in many languages, it means "must not/can't." A third structure, *must*, will be introduced in Lesson 8, but this is far less common than the forms presented here and is usually used to indicate an obligation coming from a third person.

SPEAKING AND SOUNDS

1. **Aim: to present *have to* and *have got to*; to infer context.**

● Write the sentences on the board and ask the students to say who is speaking and to whom. There are many possibilities, so encourage the students to use their imaginations. Ask the students to try to say *why* these things are necessary.

> **Possible Answers**
> 1. A parent to a child in a car.
> 2. A flight attendant to a passenger on a plane.
> 3. A bartender to a customer.
> 4. A parent to a child.
> 5. A flight attendant to a passenger on a plane.
> 6. Father or mother to daughter's boyfriend.

2. **Aim: to focus on pronunciation of *have to* and *have got to* in relaxed speech.**

● In normal, relaxed speech, the pronunciation of *to* becomes very weak, and the syllable blends with the preceding verb. Ask the students to say the words in the list.

● 🔲 Ask the students to listen and decide which they hear, /ˈgɒtə/, /ˈhæftə/, or /ˈhæstə/.

> **Answers**
> 1. a   2. b   3. b   4. a   5. b   6. c

GRAMMAR

1. **Aim: to practice using *have to*, *have got to*, and *don't have to*.**

● Ask the students to read the information in the grammar box and then complete the sentences.

● Some of the students' answers to this exercise will depend on their point of view or experience, but this might provide an interesting topic for discussion.

> **Possible Answers**
> 1. You **have got to** work hard to learn a foreign language.
> 2. I **have to** go shopping. We're out of milk.
> 3. You **have got to** be 21 years old to go into a bar in the United States.
> 4. I **have to** get up at 5:00 every morning.
> 5. You **don't have to** be a woman to take care of children.
> 6. You **don't have to** go to the bank—I'll lend you some money.

2. **Aim: to personalize the use of the target structures.**

● Ask the students to think of five or six things that they have to do this week. You may like to suggest these areas to think about: *at home, at work, at school, repairs and maintenance, health, family*. Then ask them to write sentences using *have (got) to*.

3. **Aim: to provide further practice using *have to*, *have got to*, and *don't have to*.**

● Tell the students to work in small groups and compare their lists of things to do by asking questions based on their own lists. As a group, they should decide who has the busiest week, and why.

READING

1. **Aim: to read for main ideas.**

● Ask the students to read the rules and match them with the pictures. Even if they are unfamiliar with some of the vocabulary in the text, they should be able to guess the meaning from the illustrations.

> **Answers**
> Picture 1: Always stop to pick up hitchhikers.
> Picture 2: Never use a cell phone while you're driving.
> Picture 3: Always drive as close as possible to the car in front of you.
> Picture 4: Always wear a seat belt and a helmet.
> Picture 5: Always pull over if there is an emergency vehicle behind you.

2. **Aim: to react to the text and practice using the target structures.**

● Some of the "rules" about driving in the United States are true, others are false, and others are merely advisable. Ask the students to agree with those that are true, and correct those that are false.

> **Answers**
> True. **You have to** drive on the right side of the road in the United States.
> False. **You have to** keep back from the car in front.
> True. **You have to** stop at a red light.
> False. **You have to** wear a seatbelt, **but you don't have to** wear a helmet.
> False. Many people use a cell phone while they are driving, but it is not a good idea.
> True. **You have to** take a taxi or ask a friend to drive when you have been drinking alcohol.
> False. **You don't have to** stop to pick up hitchhikers. It can be dangerous.
> True. **You have to** pull over if there is an emergency vehicle behind you.

VOCABULARY AND LISTENING

1. **Aim: to present the words in the vocabulary box.**

● Ask the students to match the words in the box and the situations. Some words can go with more than one situation.

> **Answers**
> **on the freeway:** passenger, driver's license, insurance, drunk, police officer, fine, speed limit, registration, ticket
> **at the airport:** bag, baggage, check-in, security, Walkman, passenger, laptop, batteries, pack, ticket
> **in a bar:** ID, drunk
> **on a bus:** Walkman, passenger, guide dog, ticket

2. **Aim: to practice talking about obligation.**

● Ask the students to work in pairs and discuss what they have to and don't have to do in the situations in activity 1. You may like to do this orally.

> **Possible Answers**
> **on the freeway:** You have to drive safely and not too fast.
> **at the airport:** You have to arrive one hour before the plane leaves. You have to have a plane ticket. You have to check in.
> **in a bar:** You have to show ID. You don't have to drink alcohol.
> **on a bus:** You have to buy a ticket. You have to sit down.

3. **Aim: to listen for main ideas.**

● 🔲 Ask the students to listen and decide what the situations are.

> **Answers**
> **Conversation 1:** on the freeway
> **Conversation 2:** on a bus
> **Conversation 3:** at the airport

4. **Aim: to practice using *have (got) to*; to listen for specific information.**

● Ask the students to think about what the people have to do.

> **Answers**
> **Conversation 1:** He has to drive more slowly. He has to pay a big fine.
> **Conversation 2:** She has to get off the bus.
> **Conversation 3:** He has to open his bag. He has to take the batteries out of his walkman and laptop.

● 🔲 Play the tape again. Pause after each conversation to check the answers.

5. **Aim: to practice using *have to* and *don't have to*; to describe a job.**

● Ask the students to think about a job, and describe what you have to do in this job. They should not tell anyone what the job is.

● Ask them to tell the class the "rules" for that job, starting with the least obvious, until someone guesses correctly what the job is.

7

GENERAL COMMENTS

Modal verbs

The focus of this lesson is modal auxiliary verbs. Modal verbs have a number of points in common, which are mentioned in the grammar box. Most of them have a number of different meanings and uses. For example, in this lesson, *can* is used to talk about ability, whereas in Lesson 8 it is used to talk about permission and prohibition. Lessons 8 through 10 in continue the work on modal verbs.

Can and *could* (1) for ability

This use of *can* is likely to have been covered at an earlier stage in the students' English lessons. In this context, *can* means *know how to* and refers to a general ability. You can also use *can* to express possibility, permission, and prohibition. Some languages do not use the same verb to express these different functions. The use of *could* is complex. You can use it in affirmative sentences to talk about general ability in the past, e.g. *I could read when I was six,* but not usually for a particular ability in the past. In this case, you use *was/were able to,* e.g. *There was no traffic on the way to the station so I was able to catch my train.* The exception is when *could* is followed by *see* and *hear,* e.g. *It was cloudy and I could see it was raining in the distance.* You can use *couldn't* in negative sentences to talk about a general or a particular ability in the past, e.g. *I couldn't swim when I was five. I'm sorry, I couldn't get here earlier.*

Pedagogic and real-life motivation

Choosing material which you think the students will find interesting is one way of creating motivation. *The Skylight* was chosen for its interest and dramatic tension, but in the classroom even strong material needs the pedagogic motivation of tasks to captivate the students' interest until real-life motivation takes over. The story is divided into four parts, because the length of a listening passage can compromise motivation, and each part has a different task to be done while listening, except for the fourth part, when it is hoped that students will be listening because they are genuinely interested and real-life motivation has taken over.

SPEAKING

1. Aim: to practice using *can* for general ability.
- Ask one or two students which things they can do. Some of them may appear strange, but will be useful when the students use *could* in *Grammar* activity 1.

- Ask the students to go around and find people who can or can't do the things mentioned in the list.

- Ask the students to find other things they can or can't do. You may want to write the following prompts on the board: *read Japanese, speak German, tell lies, repair your car, sleep ten hours.*

2. Aim: to practice using *can* for general ability.
- Explain that you can use *So can I / Nor can I* if you can or can't do the same things and *Can you? I can't* if you can't do the same things.

GRAMMAR

1. Aim: to focus on *could* for general ability in the past.
- Ask the students to read the information about *can* and *could* in the grammar box.

- Ask the students to think about what they could do in the past when they were five years old, and to write some sentences.

2. Aim: to practice using *could* for general ability in the past.
- Ask the students to go around asking and saying what they could do in the past.

- Find out what things people could do in the past but can't do in the present.

LISTENING AND SPEAKING

1. Aim: to prepare for listening and to pre-teach some important words from the story.
- Explain that the story is about a mother and her five-year-old son, and that they are going on holiday. A *skylight* is a small window in a roof. You can see one in the illustration.

- Ask the students to work in pairs and to use the words to predict what is going to happen in the story. Because this activity is designed to pre-teach some important vocabulary, they may need to use their dictionaries or ask you to explain any unfamiliar words. Try to limit the explanations to five or six words.

2. Aim: to practice listening for main ideas.
- This activity is designed to help the students check their predictions. They are not asked to understand every detail. Make sure that everyone knows the meaning of the word *skylight*. Play the tape.

- Ask one or two students to retell the story. Check that everyone has understood the main points. If necessary, play the tape a second time.

3. Aim: to check comprehension and to prepare for listening.
- Give the students time to read the questions.

- Ask the students to predict what is going to happen in the second part of the story. Do this activity orally with the class as a whole.

4. Aim: to listen for main ideas.

● 📼 Ask the students to listen to the second part of the story and to check their answers to the questions in activity 3. Play the tape.

Answers
1. Because it was locked.
2. The skylight.
3. She climbed up a ladder.
4. She didn't.
5. Johnny.
6. To go downstairs and unlock a window.
7. No.

5. Aim: to prepare for listening.

● Ask the students to complete the missing words and phrases from the tapescript of part 3 of the story. They can do this individually or in pairs.

6. Aim: to listen for specific information.

● 📼 Ask the students to listen and check their answers to activity 5. Play the tape.

Answers
name, car, stop, cry, around, road, door, happened, car, house, lane

7. Aim: to prepare for listening; to predict the end of the story.

● Ask the students to work in pairs and to predict the end of the story.

● Ask the students to tell the rest of the class what they think is going to happen.

8. Aim: to pre-teach some important vocabulary; to listen for main ideas.

● Check that everyone understands the key items of vocabulary.

● 📼 Play the tape.

● Ask the students how they would feel in the woman's position at the end of the story.

VOCABULARY

1. Aim: to focus on the words in the vocabulary box.

● Most of the listening activities accompanying the story were concerned with the main ideas, and no special attention was given to the vocabulary. The words in the box represent the items which are most useful at this level, but you may want to exploit more vocabulary from the story. Ask the students to reconstitute the story using the words in the box. Ask one student to start telling the story. If anyone thinks he or she has missed something out, they can ask a question. If the first person can answer the question, he or she continues telling the story. If he or she can't answer the question, the person who asked the question takes over.

2. Aim: to encourage vocabulary acquisition according to personal categories.

● Ask the students to think of categories of their own choice which they can use to organize the new words. They may like to put the words into different categories in their *Wordbanks*.

● If time is short, the students may like to do this for homework.

8

GENERAL COMMENTS

Can and can't (2) for permission and prohibition

This is the second lesson on *can*. Some students may be confused that you can use the same verb for talking about permission and prohibition, and for describing general ability. If so, write *can* on the board and underneath write *know how to* and *be allowed to*. Some students may have used *can't* in Lesson 6 for prohibition. It has the same meaning as *must not* in this context, and the only reason it was not introduced in Lesson 6, was in order not to overload the students with too many structures.

Cross-cultural awareness

If you are teaching a mono-cultural group, the answers to the questions in *Breaking the Rules?* are all likely to be very similar. In the listening passage, an American talks about the rules and customs in the United States in order to create the opportunity of cross-cultural comparison. It is not assumed that the students need to acquire this information about the United States because they are going to visit the country. This is simply an opportunity to draw attention to the fact that people do things differently in different countries, and that it should not be assumed that the rules and customs in one country can be transferred to another cultural context.

READING

1. **Aim: to prepare for reading.**
- The photos show signs of rules and customs in different countries. Ask the students where they might see the signs.

> **Answers**
> No Smoking Please: in a restaurant
> Don't Even Think of Parking Here: in the street
> Clean up after your dog: in a park; in the street
> Don't Walk: in the street

2. **Aim: to read and answer the questions.**
- The passage is a kind of questionnaire, in which direct interaction is established with the reader. Ask the students to read and think about the answers for their country.

- With a multi-cultural group, you may want to discuss the answers to the questions immediately. With a mono-cultural group, in which all the answers are likely to be similar, explain that there will be an opportunity in the *Listening* section to compare rules and customs in their country with those in the United States.

GRAMMAR

1. Aim: to practice using *can* and *can't*.

● Ask the students to read the information about *can* and *can't* in the grammar box.

● Ask the students to use *can* or *can't* to make true statements about their countries.

2. Aim: to practice using *can* and *can't*.

● Ask the students to discuss their answers to activity 1 in pairs.

● You may like to check the answers with the whole class.

SOUNDS

1. Aim: to focus on strong and weak pronunciation of *can* and *can't*.

● When *can* is at the end of the sentence, it is pronounced /kæn/. When it is in the middle of a sentence, it is unstressed and pronounced /kən/. *Can't* is pronounced /kænt/. Ask the students to say the sentences out loud and decide if the sound is /æ/ or /ə/.

● ▭ Ask the students to listen and check their answers.

> **Answers**
> **Can I come in?**
> The underlined sound is /ə/.
> **Yes, you can. You can sit down there.**
> The first underlined sound is /æ/, the second is /ə/.
> **Can I smoke?**
> The underlined sound is /ə/.
> **You can't smoke in here, but you can smoke outside.**
> The underlined sounds are /æ/.

2. Aim: to focus on the pronunciation of *can* and *can't*.

● ▭ In spoken American English, it is very often difficult to distinguish between *can* and *can't* as they are both pronounced with the letter *a* in the strong form /æ/ and the /t/ sound may be assimilated with the next sound. If the word is at the end of the sentence, the /t/ ending may be clearer. Ask the students to listen and check the sentence they hear.

> **Answers**
> You can't smoke.
> You can go into the bar.
> You can't cross now.
> You can go.

LISTENING

1. Aim: to listen for main ideas.

● ▭ Explain to the students that they are going to listen to an American answering the questions in *Breaking the Rules?* Remind the students that they may not understand every word, but they should understand enough to do the task successfully.

> **Answers**
> 1. no 2. no 3. no 4. no 5. yes 6. yes

2. Aim: to practice talking about rules and customs.

● Make sure you check the answers to the questions with the students.

● Ask the students to work in pairs and say if the rules and customs are the same in the United States as they are in their countries.

● Ask the whole class for their reactions. Is there anything they find surprising? Go through each point and ask them to remember as much detail as possible.

● ▭ Play the tape a second time.

VOCABULARY AND SPEAKING

1. Aim: to practice using *can* and *can't* for permission and prohibition; to present the words in the vocabulary box.

● Explain that the words in the vocabulary box are all situations in which there may be some special rules and customs. Write sentences on the board such as *You can't smoke in church. You can walk across the road at a crosswalk.* Ask the students to make sentences with *can* and *can't* using the words.

2. Aim: to practice using *can* and *can't* for permission and prohibition.

● Ask the class what rules and customs there are in their countries. You may like to ask them to write sentences about this for homework.

9

GENERAL COMMENTS

Should

You use *should* to make suggestions, give advice, and talk about duty, perhaps in a subjective way,
e.g. *You really shouldn't work so hard. You should spend more time with your family.*

Vocabulary load per lesson

It is important for the students to realize that in real-life language situations, they will have to confront many items of vocabulary which they don't understand. In the classroom, a certain amount of vocabulary needs to be explained in order to gain access to the main ideas of a passage or to perform a given task. But it is vital not to use a reading passage as a resource for vocabulary building. Students must be encouraged to accept that some of the gaps in their understanding will not be filled by the dictionary, or by your own explanations. Try to limit the number of words you explain or the students write down in a lesson. Most students will have difficulty in retaining more than ten or twelve new words per lesson. In *Move Up* Pre-intermediate the vocabulary boxes focus on about twenty words per lesson, but it would be difficult to retain all of them in one go.

READING

1. **Aim: to prepare for reading.**
- Ask the students to think about the title of the passage and to predict why flying may be bad for your health.

- Ask the students to predict any words that are likely to be in the passage.

- You may decide to pre-teach some difficult items of vocabulary before they read. Limit them to no more than six or seven.

2. **Aim: to read for specific information.**
- The task is for the students to read the passage and find out how the information concerns them personally.

3. **Aim: to read for specific information.**
- Ask the students to re-read the passage and to focus on all the reasons why flying is bad for people's health. You may like to do this activity orally with the whole class and write a list of the reasons on the board.

> **Answers**
> less oxygen, sitting still, dehydration, jet lag, stress, and high blood pressure

GRAMMAR

1. Aim: to practice giving advice.
- Ask the students to read the information about *should* and *shouldn't* in the grammar box.
- Ask them to do the activity.

> **Answers**
> 1. You should take some aspirin.
> 2. You should see a doctor.
> 3. You should go to the dentist.
> 4. You should take some medicine.
> 5. You should get some exercise.
> 6. You should lie down.

2. Aim: to practice giving advice.
- The students will have to re-read the passage again in order to get the exact answers for this task.

> **Answers**
> People who have had an operation recently shouldn't fly for ten days.
> You should get some exercise during the flight.
> You shouldn't eat or drink too much.
> You shouldn't drink alcohol.
> You should change to your new time zone as soon as possible.
> You shouldn't sleep if it's still daylight.

VOCABULARY

1. Aim: to focus on the words in the vocabulary box; to practice giving advice.

> **Answers**
> If you are nauseous, you should lie down and you shouldn't eat anything.
> If you are sick, you should go to the doctor.
> If you are sore, you should rest or take some aspirin.
> If you are thirsty, you should have something to drink.
> If you are tired, you should go to bed.

2. Aim: to focus on the words in the vocabulary box.
- Ask the students to group the words under the headings.

> **Answers**
> **parts of the body:** arm, ear, head, heart, leg, lung, nose, stomach, throat
> **medical conditions:** ache, cold, disease, fever, flu, hangover, high blood pressure, insect bite, jet lag, pain, sunstroke
> **Words which go together:** earache, headache, stomachache, heart disease, lung disease

- You may like to review some of the vocabulary presented in Lesson 1 on parts of the body.

LISTENING

1. Aim: to prepare for listening.
- The listening passage is quite complex and dense, so it is a good idea to help the students predict as much of the passage as possible, and then listen in order to check their predictions.

2. Aim: to listen for specific information.
- 📼 Play the tape and ask students to check their answers to activity 1.

> **Answers**
>
> | complaint | advice |
> | --- | --- |
> | jet lag | Drink a lot of water. Try to stay awake. |
> | upset stomach | Drink only bottled or boiled water. Don't eat uncooked food. |
> | insect bites | Use an insect repellent. Cover your arms and legs in the evening. Wear a hat. |
> | sunstroke | Don't spend all day in the sun. Wear a hat. |

3. Aim: to practice speaking and to listen for specific information.
- Ask the students to try to remember as much detail as possible about the doctor's advice. Ask the following questions and elicit suitable answers:
  Why should you drink a lot of water?
  Why should you try to stay awake?
  Why shouldn't you eat uncooked food?
  Why should you drink only bottled or boiled water?
  Why should you use an insect repellent?
  Why should you cover your arms and legs in the evening?
  Why should you wear a hat?
  Why shouldn't you spend all day in the sun?

- 📼 Play the tape again and ask them to listen and check.

SPEAKING

Aim: to practice speaking.
- Ask the students to think about dangers to health in their country, and to make a list of things you should or shouldn't do. They may like to discuss their advice, or write it down for homework.

10

GENERAL COMMENTS

Asking for permission; asking people to do things; offering

The language functions in this lesson use many of the modal verbs and other structures which have already been presented in *Move Up* Pre-intermediate. The grammar will, therefore, be largely review but the language functions may be new. For some students, it is a common mistake to use an infinitive after a modal. Remind them, if necessary, that modal verbs do not take an infinitive.

Cross-cultural training

The aim of the questionnaire is not to encourage students to adopt American customs, but to focus on the students' own way of doing things, to compare this with customs and behavior in other countries, and to draw attention to any differences, particularly anything which may cause offense or be perceived as offensive. Even in a mono-cultural group, there are likely to be some different answers to these questions, so take the opportunity to help students to reflect on their own culture, customs, and behavior. The subject is likely to generate a great deal of discussion.

READING AND LISTENING

1. Aim: to read and answer a questionnaire.
● Ask the students to read the questionnaire and answer the questions.

● There are a number of aspects of behavior and customs which need to be commented on:
1. In some countries nowadays, people have very strong feelings against smoking. In the United States, smokers are much less common than they used to be, and the unwritten rules about smoking are particularly strong when you're a guest in someone's home. It is a situation in which the guest is expected to conform to the rules of the house, not the other way around.
2. It is sometimes difficult to decide who pays for a restaurant bill. The students should simply be aware that the convention on paying may be different from what they expect.
3. In certain countries, a telephone caller can take precedence over a visitor, who may be offended by having to wait to regain the host's attention.
4. Relations between neighbors can vary from neighborhood to neighborhood, as well as from country to country.
5. Invitations may not always be meant as a definite arrangement to get together again, but more as a vague desire to meet again in the future. Only if the invitation is taken seriously does one expect a date to be set.
6. Once again, it is important not to be rude in this situation in many countries.

2. Aim: to listen for main ideas.
● 🔲 Play the tape and ask the students to listen and find out how the two speakers answer the questionnaire.

Answers
1. a 2. b 3. b 4. b 5. b 6. a

3. Aim: to practice speaking and to listen for specific information.
● Ask the students to think about what the speakers said for each answer. Do this activity orally with the whole of the class.

● 🔲 Play the tape again for the students to check if they remembered correctly.

4. Aim: to practice speaking and to compare different customs.
● Ask the students to work together and to compare their answers with what they heard on the tape.

FUNCTIONS

1. Aim: to focus on polite questions.

● Ask the students to read the information in the functions box about asking for permission and asking people to do things.

● Ask the students to do the activity

> **Answers**
> 1. Would you mind if I left early?
> 2. Would you mind helping me?
> 3. Could you tell me what the time is?
> 4. Could you tell me what your phone number is?
> 5. Is it all right if I open the window?

2. Aim: to focus on polite replies.

> **Possible Answers**
> 1. No, not at all. Go ahead.
> 2. No, not at all. I'd be happy to.
> 3. I'm sorry, I'm afraid I can't. I don't have a watch.
> 4. Yes, of course.
> 5. I'm sorry, I'd rather you didn't. I'm a little cold.

SOUNDS

Aim: to focus on polite intonation.

● 🔲 Explain that intonation can also be used to make you sound polite in English. Ask the students to listen and decide if the speaker sounds polite or rude.

> **Answers**
> 1. Is it all right if I smoke? [polite]
> 2. Could you turn the music down, please? [rude]
> 3. Would you mind if I called you back? [polite]
> 4. Would you mind telling me your name? [rude]
> 5. Would you mind giving me your phone number?
>   [polite]

● Ask the students to say the sentences politely.

VOCABULARY AND SPEAKING

1. Aim: to present the words in the vocabulary box.

● Explain that the words come from this lesson, and ask the students to remember which words they went with.

2. Aim: to use the new words in this lesson.

● Ask the students to go around the class asking for permission to do things or asking people to do things. Make sure they use expressions from the functions box.

Fluency 2

GENERAL COMMENTS

Many cultures find it difficult to express their feelings in the open forum of the classroom. This may be because to do so would involve a loss of face. This lesson is not designed to encourage students to do something which they would not do in their own culture, and if there is resistance to discussing the subjects presented in the early stages of the lesson, pass on to the later stages which use cultural icons and cultural resonance as a substitute for sources of more personal feelings. Cultural icons are objects, symbols, and concepts which have some cultural resonance, which are regarded as some form of embodiment of a particular idea in a culture. Colors, numbers, and various objects may have symbolic importance in one culture, and a different meaning in another.

VOCABULARY

1. **Aim: to present the words in the vocabulary box; to practice speaking.**
- It is likely that the students will have come across these vocabulary items in earlier stages of their English lessons. If not, you may have to explain them carefully, or translate them.

- Ask the students when they are likely to experience the feelings represented by the adjectives.

2. **Aim: to practice using the words in the vocabulary box.**
- Ask the students to work in pairs and to talk about their answers to 1.

- Ask three or four students to report their discussions to the whole class.

SPEAKING AND LISTENING

1. **Aim: to practice listening for main ideas.**
- The words presented in the vocabulary box will be used in the listening passage, so the preceding activities will also be a preparation for listening.

- 🔲 Play the tape and ask the students to put the number of the speaker by the photo he or she is talking about.

Answers
1. The kittens (bottom right-hand photo)
2. Rainy day (top right-hand photo)
3. Birthday cake (middle photo)
4. Subway (top left-hand photo)
5. View over a street (bottom left-hand photo)

2. **Aim: to practice speaking; to give an opportunity for a second listening.**
- Ask the students to work in pairs and to try to remember as much detail as possible about what each speaker said.

- Ask the students for details about what the speakers said, and write them on the board.

- 🔲 Play the tape again and ask the students to check the details.

3. **Aim: to practice speaking.**
- Ask the students to think about the concepts and to choose adjectives from the vocabulary box to describe their feelings. If students are reluctant to talk about their feelings, try to depersonalize the discussion by saying *How do people generally feel about...?*

4. **Aim: to practice speaking; to raise cultural awareness.**
- This activity confronts socio-cultural behavior directly. Many students may not even be aware of cultural restraints on the display of emotion. Ask them to say when people might be expected to show the emotions mentioned in public.

FUNCTIONS

1. **Aim: to present the expressions in the functions box.**
- Ask the students to read the information in the functions box about expressing feelings and then to do the activity. They should think about how they answered the questions in *Speaking and Listening* activity 3, and then write full sentences using the structures suggested. You may like them to do the activities in writing or orally with the whole class.

- Most students have a problem with the *-ing/-ed* endings *I'm bored* and *I'm boring*. Take time to have a close look at the expressions, and to translate them if necessary.

2. Aim: to examine the expressions in the functions box.

● This activity invites the students to compare English with their own language. Ask the students to read the information in the functions box about reacting. They can work in pairs to find out if there are any direct translations into their own language, or simply expressions which mean more or less the same as the English.

3. Aim: to practice using the expressions in the functions box.

● Ask the students to respond to the statements using the expressions in the functions box. They should decide whether they are reacting to something bad, good, or surprising. Note that some may think, for example, that to have a lot of work at the moment is very positive; others may think it is negative.

4. Aim: to practice using the expressions in the functions box.

● ▭ Play the tape and ask the students to listen for the expressions used.

● Check this activity with the whole class.

> **Answers**
> 1. Oh, that's too bad.
> 2. What a shame!
> 3. How annoying!
> 4. Congratulations. I'm so happy for you.
> 5. You're kidding!
> 6. How terrible!

5. Aim: to practice using the expressions in the functions box.

● Ask the students to go around the class saying the statements in activity 3 and reacting to them.

VOCABULARY AND LISTENING

1. Aim: to present the words in the vocabulary box; to prepare for listening.

● Explain that different colors have different cultural connotations. This activity is to explore these differences.

● Ask the students to say what ideas and feelings they associate with the colors. Do this activity with the whole class.

2. Aim: to practice listening for main ideas.

● ▭ Play the tape and ask the students to check the color and the feeling or idea.

> **Answers**
> passion: red
> cowardice: yellow
> inexperience: green
> dullness: gray
> cold: blue
> warmth: yellow
> purity/innocence: white
> death/bad luck: black, gray
> calmness: blue
> peace: white, green
> danger: red

3. Aim: to practice speaking; to provide an opportunity for a second listening.

● Ask the students to work in pairs and to try to remember more details about what the speakers said.

● ▭ Play the tape again and ask the students to check their answers.

> **Answers**
> 1. Jan from Holland: white for weddings; black for funerals.
> 2. Bisi from Nigeria: black and gray also mean unhappiness.
> 3. Helena from England: green for naivete; blues music is kind of sad; red for danger like a red traffic light.
> 4. Miguel from Spain.

READING AND WRITING

1. Aim: to prepare for reading.

● Ask the students to talk about the symbolic value of the words listed. They will have different meanings in different cultures.

● Do this activity with the class as a whole.

2. Aim: to practice reading for main ideas; to compare cultures.

● Ask the students to read the comments and to compare them with the meaning of the words in their own culture. Ask them what major similarities and differences there are. Is there anything which surprises, shocks, or amuses them?

3. Aim: to practice writing.

● Ask the students to think of other objects, numbers, or colors with symbolic meaning, and to write about them.

● You may like to ask the students to do this activity for homework.

Progress Check 6–10

GENERAL COMMENTS

You can work through this Progress Check in the order shown, or concentrate on areas which may have caused difficulty in Lessons 6 to 10. You can also let the students choose the activities which they would like to or feel the need to do.

VOCABULARY

1. Aim: to focus on collocations.

● The collocations in this activity have all occurred in Lessons 6 to 10. Ask the students to match the adjectives and the nouns.

> **Answers**
> alcoholic drink, bad cold, bad manners, duty-free drink, duty-free cigarettes, heavy cold, heavy suitcase, next-door neighbor

● Ask the students to use a dictionary and to find other collocations with these adjectives and nouns.

2. Aim: to focus on headwords and meanings.

● Explain that a word may have several different meanings as well as being different parts of speech. There are likely to be different numbers of meanings depending on the dictionary you use. Ask the students if they know what meanings the words have and if the words can be different parts of speech.

● Ask the students to look the words up in their dictionaries and count the number of meanings and check the parts of speech.

3. Aim: to use some of the meanings of the words in activity 2.

> **Answers**
> 1. He held the bottle by the **neck.**
> 2. What's the **date**? Is it the 30th?
> 3. I'm tired. Let's go **back** home.
> 4. I feel **cold**. Turn the heat on.
> 5. She was the **head** of the department.
> 6. My legs **ache**.

4. Aim: to focus on strategies for dealing with unfamiliar words.

● Students need to develop the strategies for dealing with unfamiliar vocabulary in the relatively reassuring context of the classroom. Ask them to read through these strategies and to use them when they are reading a passage with some unfamiliar vocabulary.

5. Aim: to organize vocabulary records in the *Wordbank.*

● It may be necessary to remind your students that they need to record new vocabulary not just once, but in a number of different categories, in order to help the process of acquisition.

GRAMMAR

1. Aim: to review *have to* and *don't have to.*

> **Answers**
> 1. You **have to** wear warm clothes in winter.
> 2. You **don't have to** tip your teacher.
> 3. You **have to** be 18 to vote in an election.
> 4. You **don't have to** be rich to buy a car.
> 5. You **have to** drive slowly near a school.
> 6. You **have to** be quiet in a library.
> 7. You **have to** do your homework every day.
> 8. You **don't have to** pay to go into a public park.

2. Aim: to review *couldn't* and *can.*

● Remind the students that the use of *can* and *could* here is to talk about a general ability.

3. Aim: to review *can* and *can't.*

● This use of *can* and *can't* is to talk about permission and prohibition.

> **Answers**
> 1. No, you can't.
> 2. No, you can't.
> 3. No, you can't.
> 4. Yes, you can.
> 5. Yes, you can.
> 6. Yes, you can.
> 7. No, you can't.
> 8. Yes, you can.

4. Aim: to review *should(n't)* and *ought (not)*.

Possible Answers
1. You should go to bed early tonight.
2. You ought to play tennis or go swimming.
3. You shouldn't stay in bed all day.
4. You ought not to play football at your age.
5. You should learn to speak her language.
6. You ought to go to the United States or Britain.
7. You should join a club.
8. You ought not to work so much.

5. Aim: to review *can, should, have to*, and *can't*.

Answers
1. You **can't** park a car on the sidewalk.
2. You **can** cross the road at stop lights.
3. He **should** wear a tie.
4. You **have to** pass your driving test.
5. You **can't** drink and drive.
6. She **should** see a doctor.
7. Men **have to** do military service in many countries.
8. You **can't** go to nightclubs when you're sixteen.

6. Aim: to review making polite requests.
● There are many other possible answers which you may like to discuss with the students.

Possible Answers
1. Could you turn it off, please?
2. Would you mind if I smoked?
3. Could you help me, please?
4. Could you tell me where the police station is?
5. Is it all right if I borrow your book?
6. Would you mind lending it to me?
7. What's the date, please?
8. Can you speak up, please?

SOUNDS

1. Aim: to focus on /əʊ/ and /ɔɪ/.
● /əʊ/ is a difficult sound for many language students, and at this stage it isn't necessary to get it absolutely right.

Answers
/əʊ/: wrote vote know only telephone home photo
/ɔɪ/: boy noise royal unemployment

● ▭ Play the tape and pause after each word. Ask the students to say the words out loud.

2. Aim: to focus on /ʃ/, /tʃ/, and /dʒ/.
● Ask the students to put the words in three columns. You can do this activity orally with the whole class.

Answers
/ʃ/: shoe station pressure situation
/tʃ/: teacher temperature
/dʒ/: oxygen passengers stranger

● Draw their attention to the different spellings for the same sound.

● ▭ Play the tape and pause after every word. Ask the students to repeat each word.

3. Aim: to focus on polite and friendly intonation.
● Ask the students to say these sentences in a polite and friendly way. Then ask them to say them in a rude and unfriendly way.

● ▭ Play the tape and ask the students to check they are saying the sentences in a polite and friendly way or in a rude and unfriendly way.

● Ask one or two students to say one of the sentences either in a polite and friendly way or in a rude and unfriendly way. The rest of class should decide which he or she intended.

SPEAKING AND WRITING

1. Aim: to review giving advice and to practice speaking.
● Write the prompts on the board and ask the students to suggest some advice for foreign visitors to their country.

● Ask the students to work in small groups and to prepare some more advice. They should write this down.

2. Aim: to review giving advice and permission, prohibiting, and to practice writing.
● Ask the students in their groups to write some rules that foreign visitors should be aware of.

● They can pass their rules to other groups and receive a new set of rules if they all come from the same country.

3. Aim: to practice speaking.
● Ask the groups in turn to talk about their advice and rules for visitors to their country. If they all come from the same country, choose the five most useful pieces of advice and the five most important rules. If they all come from different countries, choose the most surprising rules and advice for each country.

11

GENERAL COMMENTS

Past continuous

The students' native languages may have a past continuous tense, but it may be used in a different way to the English past continuous. A typical mistake would be to use the past continuous for more permanent actions, e.g. *She was spending her childhood in Texas,* or to use the past simple for background events instead of the past continuous, e.g. *I washed my hair when there the shower went cold.* To explain the "interrupted action" use of the past continuous, mentioned in the lower part of the grammar box, a time line might be useful.

> I was washing my hair
> ↑
> when the shower went cold.

LISTENING AND SPEAKING

1. **Aim: to prepare for the listening by predicting from the picture.**

● Ask the students to work in pairs to answer the questions in activity 1. As they answer the questions, provide any vocabulary they ask for.

> **Possible Answers**
> She is standing by the porch swing on the front porch of an isolated farm.
> She is standing on the porch looking into the garden. She has her arms folded.
> She is in her 40s, has black hair, and is wearing a summer dress. She isn't wearing any shoes.

2. **Aim: to prepare for listening to the first part of the passage, and to pre-teach some important items of vocabulary from the listening passage.**

● Explain that the story is in two parts, and you are going to play the first part. The words in the list come from the first part. Ask the students to discuss the words in groups of three or four and to guess what the story is about.

● Ask each group to tell the rest of the class their version of the story. This activity can take about ten minutes to complete. The process of predicting the story is important preparation for listening, so allow plenty of time.

3. Aim: to listen for main ideas.

● 📼 Ask the students to listen to the story and check if their predictions in activity 2 were correct.
Play the tape.

● Ask the students to re-tell the story to check that everyone has understood what happened.

4. Aim: to prepare for listening to the second part of the story.

● Ask the students to continue working in their groups and to try to predict what happens from the extracts. Make it clear that the extracts are in the wrong order.

5. Aim: to listen for specific information.

● 📼 Ask the students to listen to the second part of the story and number the extracts as they are read. Play the tape.

Answers
a. Robert Kincaid pulled a pack of cigarettes from his pocket… [5]
b. "I'll be glad to show it to you, if you want." [2]
c. "There it is, just around the curve." [7]
d. "Which way?" [4]
e. "OK, I think you can squeeze in there now." [3]
f. "What am I doing?" she thought. [6]
g. "The bridge is only about two miles from here." [1]

GRAMMAR

1. Aim: to practice using the past continuous.

● Ask the students to read the information about the past continuous in the grammar box.

● Ask the students to work in pairs and ask and say what they were doing at the six times yesterday. Go around and check that they are using the past continuous correctly.

2. Aim: to focus on the difference between the past continuous and the past simple.

Answers
1. I **understood** what she said.
2. She **was having** dinner when the phone **rang**.
3. It **was raining** when he **got** into his car.
4. He **made me** a sandwich because I was hungry.
5. I **was sleeping** at my desk when my boss **came** in.
6. I **was washing** my hair in the shower when the water **went** cold.
7. The movie **started** at 7:30.
8. He **was sitting** in the chair when it **broke**.

WRITING

1. Aim: to practice writing, using the past continuous.

● Ask the students to rewrite the story from Francesca's point of view, using the past continuous and the words and extracts earlier in the lesson.

● If time is short, this would be a good activity for homework.

2. Aim: to practice speaking or writing.

● This activity is designed to give students the opportunity to write or talk about their own experiences. Encourage them to use the story from this lesson and their own retelling of the story (in *Writing* activity 1) as models.

● You may like to ask the students to write this activity for homework.

12

GENERAL COMMENTS

Past continuous (2): *while* and *when*

This is the second lesson on the past continuous and
focuses on its use with *while* and *when*. A time line may be
helpful again:

> While I was standing there,
> ↑
> a small dog ran through the gate toward me.

> I was standing there,
> ↑
> when a small dog ran through the gate toward me.

VOCABULARY AND READING

**1. Aim: to pre-teach the words in the vocabulary
box; to prepare for reading.**

● The words in the box are of limited use for the
student at pre-intermediate level. They are nevertheless
important as items to be pre-taught, which will allow
easier access to the passage. Ask the students to explain
any items they know, and then explain the meaning of
any they are unfamiliar with.

2. Aim: to read for main ideas.

● It is important for the students to understand the
storyline, so this activity is a simple task to encourage
reading for main ideas.

3. Aim: to check comprehension.

● When the students have finished reading, ask
someone to re-tell the story to check that everyone has
understood.

● Ask the students to discuss what happened to Laura.

**4. Aim: to focus on the use of dramatic words in a
story.**

● Check that the students understand the words in the
box and can use them in a sentence of their own before
they try to put them into the text.

● Ask the students to find the correct location for the
words in the story.

> **Suggested Answers**
> …when **suddenly** I looked down…
> …and **instead** I was walking down a brick path.
> **Naturally**, I was a little frightened…
> …and they were **obviously** in love…
> **Anyway**, while I was standing there…
> I **somehow** realized that he couldn't see me…

GRAMMAR

1. Aim: **to focus on interrupted actions with *while* + past continuous.**

● Ask the students to read the information about the past continuous in the grammar box.

● Ask the students to do the activity. For the most useful practice in manipulating this structure, make sure the students write full sentences.

Answers
1. While Laura was walking home late one night, she had a very strange experience.
2. While she was walking along the brick path, she saw a thatched-roof cottage.
3. While she was watching the young couple, a small dog ran through the gate toward her.
4. While she was trying to make up her mind what to do, she turned to look back the way she had just come, and there was her street again.

2. Aim: **to focus on interrupted actions with *when* + past simple.**

● Encourage the students to write full answers.

Answers
1. Laura was walking home late one night when she had a very strange experience.
2. She was walking along the brick path when she saw a small thatched-roof cottage.
3. She was watching the young couple when a small dog ran through the gate toward her.
4. She was trying to make up her mind what to do when she turned to look back the way she had just come, and there was her street again.

3. Aim: **to focus on two consecutive actions using *when* + past simple.**

● Ask the students to answer the questions.

Answers
1. When Laura looked down from the moon, everything familiar vanished.
2. When this happened, she felt a little frightened.
3. When she got closer to the cottage, she saw a young couple sitting in the garden.

SPEAKING

1. Aim: **to practice speaking.**

● Ask the students to work in pairs and share stories about people who have seen things and events from the past.

2. Aim: **to practice speaking.**

● Ask the students if they believe Laura's story. Do they think it is possible to travel in time?

● Ask one or two students where they would like to travel to in time.

● Ask them to work in pairs and to discuss their time traveling. They should talk about the time and the people they would like to meet.

3. Aim: **to practice speaking.**

● Ask the students to tell the rest of the class about their time traveling. Find out if anyone else wants to travel with them. As a class, decide who has the strangest reasons for traveling.

13

GENERAL COMMENTS

Expressions of quantity

This is the second of two lessons in *Move Up* Pre-intermediate which focus on expressions of quantity, the first one being countables and uncountables in Book A, Lesson 15. You may want to ask the students to re-read the explanation in the grammar box of that lesson, as much of the information there will be relevant to this lesson too. The structures should be simpler than those in Lessons 11 and 12, and should provide a change of tempo in the course.

READING

1. Aim: to read for specific information.
- Explain that the passage is a transcript of two eight-year-old children talking about the environment.

- Ask the students to read the passage and to note down or underline anything they think is a good suggestion and write a correction for anything which is wrong.

- When the students have finished, check their answers orally.

2. Aim: to present the target structures and to practice reading for specific information.
- The structures to be presented and practiced in the *Grammar* section can all be found in these statements. Ask the students to decide which Chelsea and Eryn would agree with. For statements which they think the children would not have an opinion about, suggest that they write a question mark.

> **Possible Answers**
> Chelsea and Eryn would probably agree with 2, 6, 7, 8, and 9. In general, they are concerned about pollution and overcrowding.

3. Aim: to focus on the target structures.
- Ask the students to check the statements they agree with. In case the students check them all, ask them to choose the three most important statements.

- Ask the whole class about their choice of statements.

GRAMMAR

1. Aim: to focus on *too, much, many,* and *enough.*
- Ask the students to read the information about expressions of quantity in the grammar box.

- Ask the students to complete the sentences.

> **Answers**
> 1. It's **too** quiet for me in the countryside.
> 2. There aren't **enough** forests in the world.
> 3. The center of my country is **too** flat. I prefer the mountains.
> 4. There are too **many** factories.
> 5. It isn't peaceful **enough** in the city.
> 6. There's **too** much pollution in the sea.

2. Aim: to focus on expressions of quantity.
- Ask the students to write sentences giving their opinions about the issues mentioned and using the expressions of quantity in the grammar box.

3. Aim: to practice using expressions of quantity.
- Ask the students to work in pairs and to talk about their opinions about the statements in *Reading* activity 2. They can use their ideas from 2 and the expressions of quantity to help them.

4. Aim: to practice using expressions of quantity.
- Ask the students to write sentences about the environment near their homes. You may need to give individual students some relevant vocabulary at this stage.

- At the end of the activity, write on the board the extra vocabulary you supplied.

VOCABULARY AND SPEAKING

1. Aim: to present the words in the vocabulary box.
- The words in the vocabulary box are all useful to talk about geographical locations, the environment, and the countryside. Ask the students to write the words which can go together.

> **Answers**
> **beach:** peaceful, noisy, quiet
> **city:** noisy, hilly, industrial, poor, quiet, rich
> **coast:** flat, hilly, mountainous, industrial, noisy, peaceful, poor, rich
> **countryside:** flat, hilly, mountainous, peaceful, quiet
> **desert:** flat
> **factory:** noisy, quiet
> **farmland:** poor, hilly, quiet, peaceful
> **field:** flat, hilly, peaceful
> **forest:** peaceful, quiet
> **island:** flat, hilly, mountainous, peaceful, rich, poor
> **jungle:** noisy, peaceful, quiet
> **lake:** flat, peaceful, quiet
> **ocean:** noisy, peaceful
> **region:** mountainous, peaceful, quiet, rich, poor, rural, industrial
> **sea:** noisy, peaceful
> **town:** noisy, hilly, flat, industrial, poor, rich

- If the students ask, you may have to explain that some words go together and others don't. For example, *countryside* suggests the physical aspect of a region, so *rich* and *poor* don't really go with it, and nor does *industrial* because if the countryside is industrial, it's no longer called the countryside.

2. Aim: to practice speaking.
- Ask the students to work in groups and make predictions about the environment. Remind them, if necessary, to use *will.* Encourage them to choose from the phrases provided.

14

GENERAL COMMENTS

The passive

Traditionally, the passive has been presented in the context of manufacturing processes. In fact, the structure occurs in many other contexts in every day language use. In this lesson, it can be found in a passage about the Day of the Dead in Mexico, in which we are interested in the events and the processes of the religious festival. Some languages do not have a passive form, and you may need to supplement the presentation in this lesson with material from the Practice Book and the Resource Pack. In the grammar box, reference is made to *by* as the agent, and you may like to add an explanation about *with* to be used for instruments which are used by the agent to perform the actions, e.g. *The bowl was filled with flowers.*

Reading

It is very common for a passage to be read by the student and used for language practice without necessarily being understood or appreciated in its own right as reading material. The main reading tasks in *Move Up* encourage the students to gain access to what might be described as the heart of the matter, or the reason why the passage was written in the first place. It is very easy for pedagogical tasks to distract the student from the pleasure of the passage. So it is only after the heart of the matter has been reached that the passage is used for more obviously linguistic purposes. In *The Day of the Dead*, activities 2 and 3 create an opportunity for the students to think about the ideas suggested by the passage. The subsequent tasks are more concerned with language learning.

READING AND VOCABULARY

1. **Aim: to prepare for reading, to present the words in the box; to pre-teach some important items from the passage.**
   - Ask the students what they know about the Day of the Dead in Mexico. If anyone has any suggestions, write any key vocabulary items on the board.

   - Ask the students to look at the words in the box and to predict which ones they are likely to see in the passage.

2. **Aim: to read for main ideas; to react to the passage.**
   - The activity is intended to help the students read and react to the text as a whole. For many cultures, the most surprising thing is that the festival is a celebration of death. It is not meant to be a sad occasion. Ask the students to read and find the strangest or most interesting piece of information in the passage.

   - Ask the students if they have experienced a religious festival like this.

3. **Aim: to read for specific information.**
   - Ask the students to re-read the passage and to decide what the photos show. They can write a short caption for each photo.

GRAMMAR

1. Aim: to practice asking questions in the passive.

● Ask the students to read the information about the passive in the grammar box.

● Ask the students to do the exercise. Suggest that they will find the "answers" in the passage; somewhere around these answers will be the information needed to write questions.

> **Possible Questions**
> 1. What is November 1 called?
> 2. What is prepared for the dead?
> 3. What is baked by the men?
> 4. What is put on the table?
> 5. What is felt by the family?
> 6. What is given to the community?

● It may be easier to do this activity orally with the whole class.

● Ask the students to write down the questions when you have finished checking orally.

2. Aim: to practice using the passive.

● You may need to point out that the agent *by* may be useful in many of the sentences if you are particularly interested in *who* or *what* performed the action.

> **Answers**
> 1. The Day of the Dead is celebrated on November 1.
> 2. A feast is prepared.
> 3. Bread is often bought in markets.
> 4. The spirit is felt by the family.
> 5. The gifts are arranged around a wooden frame.

● Check the students' answers and help them decide why the agent is or isn't necessary in each sentence.

3. Aim: to decide if a sentence should be active or passive.

● This activity is designed to help students be more aware of whether an active or a passive sentence is better. Do the activity orally.

> **Answers**
> 1. b. We are more interested in Nissan cars than who makes them.
> 2. b. We are more interested in what is sold than who sells them.
> 3. a. We are more interested in the subject, i.e. *my mother* than what she does.
> 4. a. We are more interested in *my brother* than the object of the sentence.
> 5. a. We are more interested in what is drunk than in who drinks it.
> 6. a. We are more interested in cats and one of their characteristics, than in warm beds and the fact that they attract cats.

SPEAKING AND WRITING

1. Aim: to practice using the passive in descriptions of events and processes.

● Ask the students to work on their own and to make notes on an important ritual or festival. Ask them to write a few sentences using passives.

2. Aim: to practice speaking and writing notes.

● Ask the students to go around and find out which festival or ritual other people have chosen. They should choose one festival or ritual, ask questions and make notes about it because they will have to write a passage about it in activity 3.

3. Aim: to practice writing.

● Ask the students to write a passage about their partner's festival or ritual using the notes they made in activity 2.

● You may like to ask the students to do this activity for homework.

15

GENERAL COMMENTS

Cross-cultural training

Even if your students all come from the same country or have the same cultural background, they are likely to have different answers for some of the questions. Remember that one way of becoming more sensitive to other people's cultures is to become more aware of one's own culture.

Jigsaw listening

There is a further example of jigsaw listening with one tape recorder in this lesson. For a description of the background to this technique, see the teacher's notes for Book A, Lesson 15.

Correction

The material in this lesson is likely to generate quite a lot of discussion. Use the opportunity for fluency practice, and don't worry about the students' accuracy. It is very disturbing for students if you correct them while they are involved in trying to put an idea or opinion across. Make a note of any mistakes and discuss them with the students at a later stage.

Main photo

A scene from a Marx brothers' movie, with Harpo Marx.

VOCABULARY AND READING

1. **Aim: to present the words in the vocabulary box and to pre-teach some important words.**

● Ask the students to group the words under the five headings.

> **Answers**
> **things to eat:** fries, ice cream, jelly, melon, pasta, sausage, steak, toast
> **things on the table:** bowl, cup, dish, fork, knife, napkin, plate, saucer, spoon, tablecloth, teaspoon
> **things to cook with:** fork, knife, pot, saucepan, spoon
> **parts of the body:** chin, elbow, hand, lap, neck
> **things to say when eating or drinking:** cheers

2. **Aim: to personalize and extend the vocabulary list.**

● Ask the students to think about other words to add to their lists. Ask for suggestions and write them on the board. If necessary, they can use their dictionaries.

3. **Aim: to read and answer the questions.**

● Ask the students to read the questions and think about their answers. The questions all concern aspects of behavior at the dining table or conventions concerning food. In the United States, many children are given explicit training by their parents in table manners. Other social conventions are acquired more implicitly by role modeling.

LISTENING AND SPEAKING

1. Aim: to listen for specific information.

● 📼 Ask the students to work in three groups, A, B, and C. The members in each group should look at their instructions in the Communication Activities. Each group has different questions to answer. Ask them to listen and to write notes in answer to their specific questions.

● Ask the students in each group to discuss their answers, and check that everyone has got the same information.

2. Aim: to discuss what they have heard, to reconstitute the two listening passages, and to complete the charts.

● Ask the students to form new groups of three people, with one person from group A, one person from group B, and one person from group C. They should work together and talk about the notes they made in activity 1. Remember (from Book A, Lesson 15) that the rule is that they can only talk about information which they were specifically asked to listen for and write down. Ask them to answer the questions with as much detail as possible.

● 📼 Play the tape again and ask the students to check their answers. You may like to check their answers orally.

Answers
Student A: nothing; he cuts with the fork in his left hand and the knife in his right, then puts the fork in his right hand to eat; chicken, pizza, hamburgers, sandwiches; "Well said!" after a toast..
Student B: noon for lunch, 6 P.M. for dinner; napkin on his lap or next to his plate; hands on the table
Student C: a typical meal is 30 minutes; knife and fork together in the center of his plate; never smokes.

● Point out that Carlos's answers are typical of most American people, but that many people may do things differently.

GRAMMAR

1. Aim: to focus on *but, however,* and *although.*

● Ask the students to read the information about making comparisons in the grammar box.

● Ask the students to do the activity. Explain that more than one word can be used to complete the sentences.

Answers
1. Many people have dinner early, **although/but** we eat late, at about nine.
2. Most people have milk in their tea, **although/but** I prefer lemon.
3. I hold my fork in my left hand to cut food, **although/but** I change to my right hand to eat.
4. I usually drink coffee in the morning, **although/but** I sometimes have a cup after dinner.
5. Some people put their hands in their lap. **However**, I don't.
6. You don't usually smoke while you're eating. **However**, it's OK to smoke after the meal.

2. Aim: to practice using *but, however,* and *although.*

● Ask the students to write sentences comparing table customs in their family with those of Carlos.

SOUNDS

Aim: to focus on stress and intonation in sentences with *but, however,* and *although.*

● 📼 Ask the students to listen to the sentences and notice the stress and intonation patterns. When *although* starts a sentence, the voice usually rises at the end of the clause. With *however,* the voice falls on the word. They should repeat the sentences.

SPEAKING AND WRITING

1. Aim: to practice speaking and writing.

● Divide the students into groups of three or four. Ask each group to think of a social occasion. They should write down three customs, two false and one true. Encourage them to be as creative or amusing as they like. For the false custom, they may like to describe something which you should certainly not do!

● If you have time, ask each group to prepare a little sketch incorporating the customs.

2. Aim: to practice speaking.

● Ask the students to present their customs to the rest of the class; the other students should guess which is the false information.

● If you have time, ask the students to act out the sketches they may have prepared in activity 1.

Fluency 3

GENERAL COMMENTS

Culture tends to be defined in what might be described as geo-political terms, referring to nationality or regions of the world: *the North Americans, the Southern Europeans, the Southeast Asians.* But culture crosses national and regional boundaries and embraces not simply ethnic origin but factors such as age, socio-economic background, profession, and gender. This lesson focuses on the differences in attitudes, traditions, and customs between men and women.

The language in the functions box is that of giving opinions, agreeing, and disagreeing. Some cultures find it difficult to express both their opinions or open disagreement with someone, preferring to conceal their real views and acting accordingly after agreement has apparently been reached. For some more forthright cultures, such as the North Americans, this can cause much disappointment and confusion when the truth of the matter is revealed. It may be that the language presented in the box is used mostly for receptive use.

SPEAKING AND LISTENING

1. **Aim: to present the topic of the lesson; to practice speaking.**
   - Explain that the topic of the lesson is, as the title suggests, women and men. Find out if they think the role of men and women has changed in recent years. Do they believe that one gender has more opportunities than the other? Do they believe that men have specific roles in society and women have different roles?

   - Ask the students to look at the list of words and to decide if they associate a specific gender with them.

2. **Aim: to practice speaking.**
   - Ask the students to work in pairs and to talk about the gender association of the words in 1.

   - Ask the students to report their discussions to the whole class.

3. **Aim: to practice speaking; to prepare for listening.**
   - Ask the students to talk about the gender customs in their country. Find out if they think any of these customs exist and if they are considered old-fashioned.

   - Check there are no vocabulary problems at this stage.

4. **Aim: to practice listening for main ideas.**
   - Activity 3 will have prepared the students for listening. They will not need to understand every word of what they hear, only the main ideas.

   - 🔲 Play the tape and ask students to put a check by the questions in 3 to which they answer yes.

   - Ask the students to check their answers in pairs. Play the tape again if necessary.

   > **Answers**
   > 1. Yes (50-50)
   > 2. Yes (older men)
   > 3. Doesn't say
   > 4. Yes (older men)
   > 5. Yes
   > 6. No
   > 7. No

5. **Aim: to practice speaking; to provide a model for a role play.**
   - Ask the students to work in pairs and to use the conversation as a model for a role play. They may modify the conversation if they want.

FUNCTIONS

1. Aim: to focus on when you express opinions.
● Ask the students to read the information in the functions box and then to do the activity. The answers to these questions will vary from culture to culture. Use them as a springboard for discussion.

2. Aim: to focus on the language in the functions box.
● Ask the students to decide which expressions they can translate into their own language. Point out that even in English, people are reluctant to disagree very strongly. *No way!* is an expression of very strong disagreement.

3. Aim: to practice using the language in the functions box.
● Ask the students to use the language in the functions box to express their opinions from *Speaking and Listening* activity 1. Students from some cultures may have difficulty doing this, so it would be unfair to insist, as this kind of cross-cultural training is designed not to modify behavior but to raise awareness. If students do not want to express their own opinions, they can talk about opinions in a very general way.

4. Aim: to practice using the language in the functions box.
● Ask the students to work alone and to use the language in the functions box to express their opinions about the subjects mentioned.

5. Aim: to practice using the language in the functions box.
● Ask the students to work in pairs and to use the conversation in *Speaking and Listening* activity 5 to express their opinions on the subjects in 4.

READING AND LISTENING

1. Aim: to prepare for listening.
● Ask the students to read the statements and to decide which ones they agree with. Point out that some of the statements are contentious, but deliberately so in order to elicit strong opinions about the matters under discussion.

2. Aim: to practice speaking.
● Ask the students to work in pairs and to share their opinions about the statements. Check there are no vocabulary problems.

3. Aim: to practice listening for main ideas.
● 🔲 The students should now be well-prepared for the listening passage. Play the tape and ask them to check the statements Carla agrees with.

> **Answer**
> The only statement Carla agrees with completely is *Men should help with the housework.*

4. Aim: to practice speaking; to provide an opportunity for a second listening.
● Ask the students to remember what Carla said in detail. Write these details on the board.

● 🔲 Play the tape again and ask the students to check.

WRITING

● Ask the students to write a few sentences summarizing Carla's opinions and expressing their agreement or disagreement.

● You may like to ask the students to do this activity for homework.

Progress Check 11–15

GENERAL COMMENTS

You can work through this Progress Check in the order shown, or concentrate on areas which may have caused difficulty in Lessons 11 to 15. You can also let the students choose the activities which they would like to or feel the need to do.

VOCABULARY

1. Aim: to present multi-part verbs.
- Multi-part verbs are phrasal (with adverbs) or prepositional verbs, but it is not obvious from looking at an example of a phrasal or prepositional verb which type it might be. In fact, you can often only tell what type it is by checking where you put the noun or pronoun object. Therefore, knowing the name of the type of verb is not going to help the students cope with its structural properties. In fact, in this brief explanation, only transitive phrasal verbs and prepositional verbs are presented; intransitive phrasal verbs and phrasal-prepositional verbs (e.g. *look out for, take up with*) are covered in *Move Up* Intermediate.

> **Answers**
> **come:** away, down, in, off, around, up
> **fall:** away, down, in, off
> **look:** at, away, down, in, around, up
> **pick:** at, off, up
> **stand:** at, away, down, in, up
> **take:** away, down, in, off, around, up
> **turn:** away, down, in, off, around, up
> **throw:** at, away, down, in, off, up

2. Aim: to practice using multi-part verbs.

> **Answers**
> 1. He took **off** his coat.
> 2. I picked **up** my wallet.
> 3. She fell **down** the stairs.
> 4. I threw the wrapping **away.**
> 5. He turned **around** and looked **at** me.
> 6. She stood **up** when we came **in.**

3. Aim: to focus on word order of transitive phrasal verbs.
- Multi-part verbs present two main difficulties for students. The first is that a verb's meaning is not necessarily obvious from its separate parts (*give up, stand for*). The second is that there are strict rules about the position of the objects.

> **Answers**
> 1. Don't throw **it** away. 4. He cleaned **it** up.
> 2. He turned **it** down. 5. She gave **it** up.
> 3. He took **them** off. 6. I'll find **it** out.

4. Aim: to focus on word order of prepositional verbs.

> **Answers**
> 1. She thought about **him.**
> 2. We voted for **them.**
> 3. I waited for **her.**
> 4. He looked at **it.**
> 5. She listened to **it.**
> 6. We looked after **it.**

5. Aim: to review vocabulary.
- It may be useful to go back over Lessons 11 to 15 and categorize the multi-part verbs according to the position of the objects. There are a number of multi-part verbs in Lesson 11.

GRAMMAR

1. Aim: to review *when* + past continuous.

> **Answers**
> 1. I was playing tennis when I hurt my leg.
> 2. He was walking to work when he saw his friend.
> 3. They were watching television when they fell asleep.
> 4. She was talking to me when she started to cry.
> 5. We were sitting in the yard when we heard a loud noise.
> 6. I was looking for a pen when I found some money.

2. Aim: to review *while* + past continuous.

> **Answers**
> 1. While I was playing tennis, I hurt my leg.
> 2. While he was walking to work, he saw his friend.
> 3. While they were watching television, they fell asleep.
> 4. While she was talking to me, she started to cry.
> 5. While we were sitting in the yard, we heard a loud noise.
> 6. While I was looking for a pen, I found some money.

3. Aim: to review asking questions using the past continuous.
- This activity is designed to practice the past continuous. However, it is also possible to use the past simple with these questions.

> **Answers**
> 1. What were you doing at 8 A.M. yesterday?
> 2. Who were you talking to last night?
> 3. Why were you working so hard last week?
> 4. What were you talking about this morning?
> 5. Where were you having dinner last Sunday?
> 6. Why were you laughing just now?

4. Aim: to review *too* + adjective and *not* + (adjective) *enough*.

> **Answers**
> 1. It isn't quiet enough in here.
> 2. It was too light to sleep.
> 3. I wasn't warm enough.
> 4. The region isn't rural enough.
> 5. The hotel room wasn't clean enough.
> 6. The jacket was too small.

5. Aim: to review the passive.
● Ask the students to write their own answers to these questions. Make sure they use a passive.

6. Aim: to review the passive.

> **Answers**
> 1. A lot of coffee is drunk in Seattle.
> 2. A lot of meat is eaten in Argentina.
> 3. A lot of souvenirs are bought by tourists.
> 4. Medicine is bought at the drugstore.
> 5. Your teeth are examined by the dentist.
> 6. Plastic bags are used for carrying things.

7. Aim: to review *although*.

> **Answers**
> 1. Although she likes coffee, she prefers tea.
> 2. She doesn't usually have time to eat in the mornings, although on weekends she has a large breakfast.
> 3. Although she usually has a sandwich for lunch, she sometimes has a salad when she goes out with friends.
> 4. She doesn't smoke, although she doesn't mind other people smoking in her home.

8. Aim: to review *however*.

> **Answers**
> 1. She likes coffee. However, she prefers tea.
> 2. She doesn't usually have time to eat in the mornings. However, on weekends she has a large breakfast.
> 3. She usually has a sandwich for lunch. However, she sometimes has a salad when she goes out with friends.
> 4. She doesn't smoke. However, she doesn't mind other people smoking in her home.

SOUNDS

1. Aim: to focus on /f/ and /p/.
● 📼 Some students may have difficulty in distinguishing between the two sounds. Ask them to complete these words with *f* or *p*. Then play the tape and pause after each word. Ask the students to repeat the words.

> **Answers**
> foot play fly fever price fish paper
> pot finish five page pitch front put

2. Aim: to focus on /h/.
● 📼 Ask the students to listen and check the words they hear.

> **Answers**
> 1. ear 2. hair 3. eye 4. hat
> 5. hate 6. eat 7. art 8. as

● Ask the students to say the words out loud.

3. Aim: to focus on stress in multi-part verbs.
● 📼 Ask the students to listen and repeat the sentences. Make sure they stress the verb and the particle.

READING AND WRITING

1. Aim: to focus on rules of punctuation.
● At this stage, this activity simply confirms what the students already know about English punctuation.

2. Aim: to focus on word order.
● Ask the students to read the story again and decide where the words can go in the story.

> **Answers to Activities 1 and 2**
> An American couple drove to Mexico City for a **short** vacation. They found their way to the hotel, but couldn't find anywhere to park. Finally they found a **parking** space, but by now it was dark. While they were trying to park, a **friendly** passer-by saw their American car and offered to help. "You have a meter behind you!" he shouted. So the driver moved **back** a little. The man shouted again, "You have a meter behind you!" The driver moved a little more. The Mexican waved and shouted, "You have a meter behind you!" The American, who was getting a little angry by now, suddenly reversed the car. There was a **loud** crash! The Mexican pointed at a **metal** post which was lying under the car. "I said, you had a meter behind you!"

3. Aim: to focus on word order.
● Ask the students to think of six words which could go into the story and write them down.

● Ask them to work in pairs. They should show their words to their partner and ask him or her to decide where the words can go in the story.

● If time is short you may like to give this activity for homework.

16

GENERAL COMMENTS

May and *might*

In Lesson 10 students will have come across *may* to request permission, e.g. *May I call you Mary?* In this lesson, *may* and *might* are used to talk about a specific possibility in the future, e.g. *I may come over tonight*. You don't usually use *may* and *might* in questions about possibility; the question is usually rephrased with *Do you think... + will.* The use of *can* to talk about more general possibility (*It can get very hot in the evenings*) will be covered in *Move Up* Intermediate. This use is quite close to the use of *may* and *might* in this lesson.

VOCABULARY

1. Aim: to present the words in the vocabulary box.

- Ask the students to find the words for seasons.

- Ask the students to group the other words with the seasons. The groupings will vary from country to country. The answer below is how an American might answer.

> **Answers**
> **fall:** rain, changeable, mist, fog
> **winter:** freezing, fog, frost, ice, rain, snow, wet, wind
> **spring:** changeable, flood, mild, rain, wet, wind
> **summer:** changeable, dry, humid, hurricane, lightning, storm, sun, thunder

- Ask the students to think about words needed to talk about their weather. They may like to use their dictionaries.

2. Aim: to form adjectives from nouns.

- Encourage the students to broaden their vocabulary by making adjectives from nouns. This is particularly common with words to describe the weather.

> **Possible Answers**
> sunny, stormy, rainy, icy, windy, misty, snowy, frosty, summery, foggy, thundery, wintry

GRAMMAR

1. Aim: to practice using *because* + *might* and to give advice.

● Ask the students to read the information about *might* and *may* in the grammar box.

● Ask the students to give advice and explain why. Remind them that they saw *should* for giving advice in Lesson 9.

> **Possible Answers**
> 1. You should bring an umbrella because it might rain.
> 2. You should wear warm clothes because it might be cold.
> 3. You should bring your camera because you might want to take some photos.
> 4. You should get some sunscreen because it might be sunny.
> 5. You should buy a good map because you might want to explore the countryside.
> 6. You should bring a swimsuit because you might want to go swimming.

2. Aim: to focus on the difference between possibility and certainty.

● The verb forms or the contexts in the sentences suggest an element of certainty about the arrangement or future plan.

> **Answers**
> 1. **I'm going** to Kenya next week. I've bought my ticket.
> 2. **I've booked** into a hotel. I've reserved a room at the Ambassador.
> 3. **I might go** to Lake Victoria or perhaps to the beach near Mombasa.
> 4. **I might not** spend more than a week on the coast because I want to see the National Park.
> 5. **I might go** on safari if there's space for me.
> 6. **I'm coming** home on the sixteenth. It's the day before I get married.

3. Aim: to practice using *might* to talk about possible actions in the future.

● Ask the students to write about what they might do in the situations mentioned. To help them you may like to write on the board some suggestions, e.g. *stay at home, play tennis, go skiing, light a fire, watch TV, go to the movies, go to the library, go to bed.*

READING AND WRITING

1. Aim: to provide a reason for reading the model letter, and to provide prompts for the letter writing.

● The questions are designed to provide a reason for reading the model letter which is to be used in activity 3 for letter writing. The questions will be useful prompts at that stage.

> **Answers**
> **Where might Maria like to stay?**
> "You may like to stay in youth hostels, which are pretty cheap and convenient."
> **What type of clothes should Maria bring and why?**
> "...it might be a bit cold in the evening, so bring a sweater."
> **When might be the best time to come?**
> "I think September is the best time to come."
> **What might Benita be able to do?**
> "I might be able to take some time off and come with you!"
> **What might the weather be like?**
> "It's usually quite warm, although there may be some rain, and it might be a bit cold in the evening."

2. Aim: to make notes in preparation for writing a letter.

● This stage of the activity sequence focuses on collecting information and preparing to write the letter. You may like to ask the students to do this in pairs if they come from the same country, so that they collect as many ideas as possible. This preparation stage is very important, so give them about ten minutes to do this.

3. Aim: to write a letter.

● The final stage of this activity sequence is to use the model letter, the prompt questions, and the information and ideas collected in the preceding stages to write a letter.

● The students may like to complete this activity for homework.

17

GENERAL COMMENTS

First conditional

There are many possible ways of making a conditional sentence with present and future tenses, e.g. *If you have his number, why don't you give him a call? If you see John, tell him I'm OK. If you leave butter in the sun, it melts. If you come this way, I'll tell her you're here.* But the conditional which causes many students problems is the one for likely situations and their results, where the verb in the *if* clause goes in the present simple, and the verb in the main clause in the future. The other common error in writing is leaving out the comma which separates the two clauses. This is obviously not serious, but it makes longer sentences more difficult to read. Lesson 19 covers the second conditional for unreal or hypothetical events and situations.

Help!

The theme of the lesson is emergency situations. If you ask the students to share their own experiences of emergency situations, it is important not to cause them embarrassment or distress. In communicative methodology, in which the student is invited to contribute actively both to the learning process and to the activities in class, it is very easy to transgress social conventions concerning personal feelings and privacy. The risk is similar to a cross-cultural situation in which someone causes or perceives offense where none was intended.

VOCABULARY AND SPEAKING

1. **Aim: to focus on the words in the vocabulary box, and to group the vocabulary items under the headings to help the process of acquisition.**

● The students don't need to use all of these words productively, but they may find them useful for receptive purposes if they start reading English language newspapers.

> **Possible Answers**
> **an emergency at home:** accident, ambulance, break, burglar, burn, button, catch fire, dangerous, drown, electricity, explode, fire, flood, injured, gas, ground floor, kill, plug, plug in, press, shock, steal, turn on, turn off, unplug, victim
> **a road accident:** accident, ambulance, burn, catch fire, dangerous, explode, fire, injured, kill, rescue, shock, witness, victim
> **a bomb threat:** bomb, dangerous, explode, injured, kill, package, rescue, victim
> **a mugging:** consulate, dangerous, driver's license, injured, gun, kill, mugger, passport, shock, steal, wallet, witness, victim
> **a flood:** dangerous, drown, flood, injured, rescue, victim

2. **Aim: to present the first conditional.**

● The first conditional is presented in each of these sentences. Ask the students to decide in which emergency situation they might hear the sentences. You can do this orally with the whole class.

> **Possible Answers**
> 1. an emergency at home 2. a mugging 3. a flood
> 4. a road accident 5. a bomb threat
> The pronouns probably refer to: 1. an electric cable
> 2. a bag or wallet 3. water 4. the paramedics
> 5. a package containing a bomb

GRAMMAR

1. **Aim: to focus on the first conditional.**

● Ask the students to read the information about the first conditional in the grammar box.

● Ask the students to do the exercise.

> **Answers**
> 1. e   2. c   3. d   4. a   5. b   6. f

2. **Aim: to practice using the first conditional.**

● Ask the students to write their own sentences saying what they will do in the circumstances mentioned. Check that they are using the present simple in the *if* clause, and are separating the two clauses with a comma.

SOUNDS

Aim: to focus on merged sounds.

● 🔲 The students will already know that certain words merge with other words in connected speech. Ask them to listen and mark the words the speaker links.

Answers

If you touch that, it'll explode.

If no one picks it up, I'll do it.

If you don't stop eating, you'll get a stomachache.

If you don't let go, I'll scream.

If you don't give it to me, I'll tell a police officer.

If you ask her, she'll answer.

● Play the tape again and pause after each sentence. Ask the students to say each sentence out loud.

LISTENING AND SPEAKING

1. **Aim: to listen for main ideas.**

● 🔲 The students have already discussed the topic of emergency situations, so to a certain extent they will be ready for the listening activity. Explain that the incident is in three parts, and that you're going to play the first part. Ask them to listen and decide what the emergency incident is.

Answer
A mugging.

2. **Aim: to check that everyone has understood what happened.**

● Check that everyone has understood the main ideas of the passage by asking one or two students to re-tell the story so far.

3. **Aim: to prepare for listening to the second part.**

● Ask the students to look at the extracts and to discuss what happens next.

● 🔲 Explain to the students that they should listen and number the extracts in the order they hear them. Play the tape.

Answers

…they had some good news	[1]
…now it was me who was feeling sorry	[8]
…the young man wasn't Australian	[3]
…admitted he was guilty	[5]
…the bank teller called the police	[4]
…was unemployed and had a family to look after	[7]
…a young man was trying to change some Australian money	[2]
…"I'm sorry, I'm really sorry."	[6]

4. **Aim: to prepare for listening to the third part and to practice using the first conditional.**

● Ask the students to discuss the situation and to complete the first conditional sentences.

5. **Aim: to prepare for listening.**

● Ask the students to predict how the story ends.

● 🔲 Play the tape and ask them to listen and find out if they guessed correctly.

● Ask the students if they think Kate made the right decision.

6. **Aim: to practice speaking.**

● Ask the students to talk about emergency situations they might have been in. You can also ask them to write about it for homework.

18

GENERAL COMMENTS

Would

Would is a modal verb. The students have already come across *would* + infinitive in *What would you like? I'd like a Coca Cola.*

My Perfect Weekend

The topic is a lighthearted one, and the lesson is designed to give the students some straightforward language work and some motivating skills practice before the more significant lesson on the second conditional in Lesson 19.

VOCABULARY AND SPEAKING

1. Aim: to focus on the words in the vocabulary box; to pre-teach some difficult words from the reading passage.

● Ask the students to say which is their most important single possession. Do they think it is a luxury or a necessity?

● Ask them to think about the words in the box and decide which are luxuries and which are necessities.

2. Aim: to practice talking about luxuries and necessities.

● Ask the students to discuss their answers to activity 1. You may like to do this activity orally.

● The items have been chosen to generate cross-cultural comparison in a multi-cultural group, but in mono-cultural groups, you may like to ask the students to guess which cultures or countries might consider the items to be necessities.

● Ask the students to think of other items which they consider to be necessities.

● Then ask them to talk about their necessities with the rest of the class. This is likely to generate a lot of discussion, so give them plenty of time.

READING

1. Aim: to read and react to the passage.

● Ask the students to read the passage and to match the questions and the answers.

> **Answers**
> 1. f   2. h   3. b   4. i   5. a
> 6. e   7. d   8. g   9. j   10. c

2. Aim: to prepare to use *would* for imaginary situations.

● Ask the students to prepare for *Grammar* activity 2 by thinking about how they would spend their perfect weekend.

GRAMMAR

1. **Aim: to practice writing questions with *would*.**
- Ask the students to read the information about *would* in the grammar box.

- Explain that the sentences contain answers to questions which were not used in the passage. Ask the students to write the questions.

Possible Answers
1. What sport would you play?
2. What Broadway show would you watch?
3. What music would you listen to?
4. Would you go out to eat?
5. Would you buy a newspaper?
6. When would you go back home?

2. **Aim: to practice writing sentences with *would*.**
- Ask the students to use their answers to *Reading* activity 2 and to write full sentences in answer to the questions in the passage.

- For students who finish sooner than others, ask them to write full answers to the questions they wrote in *Grammar* activity 1.

SOUNDS

Aim: to focus on merged sounds in connected speech.
- Explain that some sounds in clusters of consonants sound different or even disappear in connected speech. Ask the students to listen and notice how the *'d* is pronounced.

- Ask the students to say the sentences out loud. It isn't essential for them to pronounce these sentences accurately, but they should realize that if they do so, they will sound much closer to a native speaker, and may be easier for other people to understand.

SPEAKING

1. **Aim: to practice speaking and using *would*.**
- Ask the students to discuss their perfect weekend. They can use their answers to *Grammar* activity 2. Make sure they ask for extra information.

2. **Aim: to practice speaking and using *would*.**
- Ask the students to imagine how other people in the class would answer the questions. You can do this orally.

3. **Aim: to practice speaking and using *would*.**
- Ask the students to find out if they guessed correctly.

- The students may like to use these answers to write about the other students' perfect weekends for homework.

19

GENERAL COMMENTS

Second conditional

The second conditional was presented implicitly in Lesson 18. In this lesson it is presented more explicitly. Make sure the students realize that the second conditional is for unreal or hypothetical situations and their results, something that is imaginary or unlikely to happen. The past tense used in the main clause is not used to express past time. *If I were you,...* is a common set phrase, and *were* can also be used for the third person singular, e.g. *If he were rich, he'd...* although it is less common than for the first person singular. The *if* clause can either come at the beginning or at the end of the sentence. In this lesson, the verb in the *if* clause is in the past simple, although there are other possibilities, e.g. *If I was sitting there, I'd close the window. If you were feeling ill, you'd go home.*

The Umbrella Man

The story in this lesson was written by Roald Dahl, who died in 1990 and who was famous for his children's books and for his collections of slightly surreal short stories such as *Kiss Kiss* and *Someone like you*. His *Tales of the Unexpected* were turned into a series of short films for television, and have been seen in many countries.

Reading and Vocabulary

Try not to explain too many items of unfamiliar vocabulary. Although the story is quite long and may contain a number of new words, you are likely to spoil the students' enjoyment if you interrupt and exploit each part for vocabulary. If you do want to talk about the vocabulary, wait until the end of the story. The aim is to give fluency practice in reading, at least until everyone has finished the story.

Grammar

Exceptionally in *Move Up*, this lesson begins with the grammar focus, because *would* has already been introduced, and to present and practice the second conditional at a later stage would spoil the enjoyment of the story.

GRAMMAR

1. Aim: to present the second conditional.

● Ask the students to read the explanation in the grammar box and then do the activities. Ask them to match the two clauses and make second conditional sentences. You can do this activity orally.

> **Answers**
> 1. If I was really rich,   b. I'd give up my job.
> 2. If I won a free vacation,   a. I'd go to Jamaica.
> 3. If I lost my wallet,   d. I'd go to the police.
> 4. If I spoke English fluently, e. I'd get a better job.
> 5. If I changed my job,   f. I'd be much happier.
> 6. If I could live anywhere,   c. I'd live in New York.

2. Aim: to practice writing second conditional sentences; to prepare for reading.

● Ask the students to write sentences saying what they would do in the circumstances mentioned. The questions reflect dilemmas which confront the character in the story.

READING AND LISTENING

1. Aim: to pre-teach some difficult vocabulary from the story; to predict what is going to happen; to prepare for reading.

● Explain any words in the list that you think the students may have difficulty with, and then ask the students to work in pairs to predict what is going to happen. The amount of time you spend on this activity depends on how motivated your students appear at the time. The story is quite long, and you may need to create an artificial motivation to start reading. If the students are slow getting down to work, it may be better to spend more time predicting the story so they are carefully prepared for reading. However, if the students appear interested in reading the story, it's best to let them get on with it.

2. Aim: to check comprehension and to practice using the second conditional.

● Ask the students to react to the story and say what they would do in these circumstances. Once again, if the motivation to read on is strong, don't spend too much time on this activity. At this stage, the focus of the work is fluency in reading, rather than the accurate manipulation of the target structure.

3. Aim: to predict what is going to happen next in the story.

● Ask the students to work together and predict what is going to happen next by looking at the phrases and by numbering them in the right order. They should also guess who is speaking.

● 🔲 Ask them to listen and check their answers. Play the tape.

> **Answers**
> a. "Why don't you walk home?"
>   [5] (mother)
> b. "He's in some sort of trouble."
>   [1] (narrator)
> c. "Thank you, ma'am, thank you."
>   [8] (old man)
> d. "I've never forgotten it before,"
>   [2] (old man)
> e. "I think I'd better just give you the cab fare."
>   [6] (mother)
> f. "I would never accept money from you like that!"
>   [7] (old man)
> g. "I'm offering you this umbrella to protect you."
>   [4] (old man)
> h. "Are you asking me to give you money?"
>   [3] (mother)

4. Aim: to practice using the second conditional.

● Ask the students to say what they would do in the circumstances if they were one of the three characters. Do this activity orally and elicit suitable answers using the second conditional.

● Ask the students to predict what is going to happen next.

● Ask the students to read on and check their predictions.

5. Aim: to predict what has happened and what will happen next.

● By this stage, the students should be involved in the story and it is important not to interrupt this authentic motivation by obvious language practice. For this reason, there is no need for an artificial, pedagogical task to make them listen to the end of the story. They should be genuinely motivated to do this on their own.

VOCABULARY

Aim: to focus on the words in the vocabulary box.

● You may think there are other items you wish to draw the students' attention to. These words were selected, however, because they are probably the most useful and relevant for students at this level. The list is also a manageable number of words to learn.

WRITING

Aim: to write the story from another point of view.

● This activity involves a lot of creativity on the part of the students, but within a well-established context. Ask them to think about the story from the old man's point of view and to discuss the reasons for his behavior.

● Ask the students to write sentences telling the story from the old man's point of view.

20

GENERAL COMMENTS

Past perfect

This tense may appear to be formed in a similar way in some students' native languages but may not operate in the same way. This is a brief introduction to the tense, and if your students have difficulty using it, they may need extra practice using material from the Practice Book and the Resource Packs. It will also be covered more fully in *Move Up* Intermediate. You only use the past perfect when you are already talking about the past and need to refer to an action or event which happened even earlier than the actions and events in which you are primarily interested. As soon as you become more interested in this earlier action or event, you use the simple past.

Contractions

You may need to point out that the contracted form *'d* stands for *had* in this lesson. In Lessons 18 and 19 it stands for *would*. The context usually makes this clear.

VOCABULARY AND READING

1. **Aim: to present the words in the box; to predict what the story is going to be about; to prepare for reading.**

● Write the words in the box on the board. Ask the students to work in groups of four or five and try to predict what the story is going to be about.

● Ask a volunteer from each group to tell the class about his or her group's predictions.

2. **Aim: to read for main ideas.**

● Ask the students to read the first part of the story and see if their predictions were correct.

GRAMMAR

1. **Aim: to focus on the sequence of events with *when*.**

● Ask the students to read the information about the past perfect in the grammar box.

> **Answer**
> *a. Wa ran away when the chief's son arrived* means that first the chief's son arrived, then Wa ran away.
> *b. Wa had run away when the chief's son arrived* means that first Wa ran away, and then the chief's son arrived; in other words, Wa was no longer there when he arrived.

2. **Aim: to focus on the use of the past perfect.**

● Ask the students to do the activity.

> **Answers**
> 1. Wa was an orphan because her parents **had died** when she was younger.
> 2. She worked hard, but the chief **didn't give** her enough to eat.
> 3. In the evening her hands were blistered because she **had worked** so hard.
> 4. She wanted to eat the rice because she **was** hungry.
> 5. The chief's son **shouted** at her.
> 6. The maiden told Wa that the Water Spirit's daughter **was** very ill.

3. **Aim: to focus on the sequence of tenses.**

● Ask the students to do the activity.

> **Answers**
> 1. Because she had worked so hard.
> 2. After the chief's son had arrived.
> 3. Because the chief had told her not to.
> 4. Because she had fallen asleep.
> 5. After Wa had bent down to fill the pail.
> 6. Because a scorpion had stung her.

LISTENING

1. Aim: to prepare for listening; to predict what is going to happen next in the story.

● Ask the students to work together and predict what is going to happen next by looking at the phrases and by trying to number them in the right order. They should also guess who is speaking.

● 🔲 Ask them to listen and check their answers. Play the tape.

> **Answers**
> a. "Get your swords," he shouted to his guards.
>   [4] (chief)
> b. "I hate you. Go away!"
>   [3] (Wa)
> c. "Pearl, wonderful pearl, protect us from this evil man."
>   [6] (Wa)
> d. "I w-w-wish to m-m-marry you!"
>   [2] (chief's son)
> e. "This pearl will make every wish come true."
>   [1] (Water Spirit)
> f. "We will go and kill that girl!"
>   [5] (chief)

2. Aim: to check comprehension of the story; to practice using the past perfect.

● Ask the students to work in pairs and answer the questions about part 2 of the story. Encourage them to use the past perfect where possible in their answers.

> **Answers**
> 1. Because Wa had cured her daughter.
> 2. Because the birds had eaten half of the rice.
> 3. Because he had seen her new house.
> 4. Because Wa had insulted his son.
> 5. She asked the pearl to protect her.

SOUNDS

Aim: to focus on merged sounds in connected speech.

● 🔲 Explain that it is sometimes difficult to distinguish between a past simple and a past perfect in connected speech, because the contracted *'d* often merges into the following sounds. Play the tape and ask the students to check the sentences they hear.

> **Answers**
> 1. She worked long and hard.
> 2. She jumped up in fear.
> 3. She'd reached the shore.
> 4. A scorpion had stung her.
> 5. He'd heard that she was back.

● 🔲 Ask the students to repeat the sentences. They should try to merge the *'d* sound into the sound which follows. You can play the tape again and pause after each sentence so that the students can say it out loud.

SPEAKING AND WRITING

1. Aim: to predict the end of the story.

● Ask the students to work together and predict the end of the story. Ask them what they would do if they were Wa.

2. Aim: to read the end of the story.

● By now the students should be motivated enough to read the end of the story without having to perform an accompanying task.

3. Aim: to write notes about a folk tale.

● Ask the students to think about a well-known folk tale from their country. If the students are all from the same country, ask them to think about a regional folk tale.

● Ask them to make notes about the main details of the story.

4. Aim: to practice speaking.

● Ask the students to work in pairs and to tell each other the folk tale, using their notes. Encourage the listeners to ask questions about anything they don't understand, as they will have to write down their partner's story in the next activity.

5. Aim: to write a story from memory and using notes.

● Ask the partners to exchange the notes they made in activity 3 and write down the story they have just heard. They may use their partner's notes, but they should not ask any more questions about the story at this point.

● You may like to ask the students to do this for homework.

Fluency 4

GENERAL COMMENTS

This final Fluency lesson in *Move Up* Pre-intermediate examines concepts and values which underlie one's cultural identity. Remind the students that when they are exposed to examples of American culture and values, they are not being invited to adopt and alter their views and behavior accordingly. They are presented as an opportunity to stimulate discussion, to reflect on their own culture, and to learn that other cultures think and behave in different ways.

One of the aims of *Move Up* is to provide students with opportunities to examine cultural similarities and differences. This may lead to stereotyping, though it should not lead to prejudices against a culture as a whole.

SPEAKING AND LISTENING

1. **Aim: to practice speaking; to practice reading and answering a quiz; to prepare for listening.**
- This quiz should provide some rich stimulus for discussion. Ask the students to work alone for the moment and to think about their answers to the quiz.

- Make sure there are no vocabulary problems.

2. **Aim: to practice speaking; to prepare for listening.**
- Ask the students to talk about their answers to the quiz.

- You may like to invite students to share their opinions with the rest of the class.

3. **Aim: to practice listening for main ideas.**
- By now the students should be well prepared for the listening passage. Remind them they will not need to understand every single word, just the main ideas.

- 📼 Play the tape and ask the students to check the questions the speaker answers.

> **Answers**
> The questions she answers are: *2, 3, 5,* and *8.*

4. **Aim: to practice speaking; to provide an opportunity for a second listening.**
- Ask the students to remember in detail what the speaker says. You may like to write these details on the board.

- 📼 Play the tape again and ask the students to check the details.

5. **Aim: to practice reacting to a text.**
- These comments reflect a variety of aspects about American culture. Ask the students to read them and to decide if any surprise or shock them.

- Ask the students for their reactions to the comments. Ask them what generalizations can be made about the statements.

6. Aim: to practice listening for main ideas.

● 🔲 Play the tape and ask the students to check the comments Gloria and Ruben agree with.

Answers

The comments they agree with are:

"I always lock the door when I leave the house, even for a short time."

"We usually watch TV during meals."

"We don't usually visit friends without an invitation."

"I don't wear a suit, except on very formal occasions."

FUNCTIONS

1. Aim: to practice using the language in the functions box.

● Ask the students to read the information in the functions box about giving instructions and advice. Then ask them to rewrite any statements in *Speaking and Listening* activity 5 which they agree with, using the language in the functions box.

2. Aim: to practice using the language in the functions box.

● Ask the students to write instructions and advice for the issues suggested.

● You may like to ask the students to work in pairs for this activity.

READING AND SPEAKING

1. Aim: to practice reacting to a text.

● *You and Us* was written by a German woman. Ask the students to read it and to decide which values it ascribes to the Americans, and which to her culture.

● Then ask them to think about which thoughts and feelings they share or agree with, either as individuals or generally within their own culture. You may like to ask students to work in pairs or small groups to discuss this, and to share their opinions.

2. Aim: to practice speaking; to review the language presented in the Fluency lessons.

● This is a final review of the language in the Fluency lessons of Parts A and B of *Move up* Pre-intermediate. Ask the students to work in pairs and to act out the situations. Remind them to look back at the relevant lessons.

● Ask two or three pairs to act out the situations in front of the class.

3. Goodbye and good luck!

Progress Check 16–20

GENERAL COMMENTS

You can work through this Progress Check in the order shown, or concentrate on areas which may have caused difficulty in Lessons 16 to 20. You can also let the students choose the activities which they would like to or feel the need to do.

VOCABULARY

1. Aim: to focus on idiomatic phrases with *do* and *make.*
● The students will have realized that *do* and *make* are very common words in English. Their native language may not make a distinction between the two: in this case, they may find this activity useful. Ask the students to use a dictionary and decide whether you use *make* or *do* with the words and phrases.

> **Answers**
> **make:** an appointment, an arrangement, a cake, notes, friends, a decision, a cup of coffee
> **do:** damage, your best, the ironing, someone a favor

2. Aim: to focus on the formation of adverbs.
● The students have already come across certain adverbs in *Move Up* Pre-intermediate. In Book A, Lesson 2, adverbs of frequency (*always, sometimes, occasionally,* etc.) were presented. This activity focuses on how to form adverbs from adjectives.

> **Answers**
> culturally, locally, slowly, quickly, heavily, quietly, expensively, beautifully, interestingly, formally, fashionably, healthily, nervously, politely, happily

3. Aim: to practice using adverbs.
● The students should use the adverbs they formed in activity 2 for this activity. Remind them that adverbs go with a verb, and adjectives go with a noun.

> **Possible Answers**
> 1. The rain fell very **heavily**.
> 2. She was singing very **beautifully/nervously**.
> 3. He dressed very **fashionably**.
> 4. He spoke kind of **quietly**.
> 5. It was raining, so we drove very **slowly**.
> 6. We live **locally**, not far from here.

4. Aim: to review the vocabulary presented in *Move Up.*
● In this last lesson of *Move Up* Pre-intermediate, ask the students to spend ten or fifteen minutes looking through all the vocabulary boxes in the book, looking for ten or twelve words which they have forgotten. They should write them down.

● Ask the students for the words they have written down and write them on the board. Ask other students to explain the words.

GRAMMAR

1. Aim: to review *might (not).*

> **Answers**
> 1. It might rain today.
> 2. I might stay a week.
> 3. She might not call me tonight.
> 4. The plane might not leave on time.
> 5. He might arrive soon.
> 6. It might be less noisy.

2. Aim: to review *may (not).*
● Ask the students to write sentences saying what they may or may not do on the weekend.

3. Aim: to review the first conditional.

> **Answers**
> 1. If you leave now, you'll catch the bus.
> 2. If you stay in bed, you'll feel better.
> 3. If you work hard, you'll get a good job.
> 4. If you eat carrots, you'll be able to see in the dark.
> 5. If you go shopping, you'll spend a lot of money.
> 6. If you ride a bike, you'll save energy.

4. Aim: to review asking questions with *would.*

> **Answers**
> 1. Where would you go?
> 2. What would you do in the morning?
> 3. Where would you go in the afternoon?
> 4. How would you get there?
> 5. What would you do in the evening?
> 6. When would you go home?

5. Aim: to review writing sentences with *would.*
● Ask the students to write answers to the questions they wrote in activity 4.

6. **Aim: to review the second conditional.**

Answers
1. f   2. b   3. d   4. e   5. a   6. c

7. **Aim: to review the second conditional.**
● Ask the students to write sentences saying what they would do in the circumstances mentioned.

8. **Aim: to review the past simple and the past perfect.**

Answers
1. After I had left the office, I went straight home.
2. When they arrived at the station, they had missed the train.
3. She walked slowly because she had hurt her ankle.
4. He wrote to me after he had had the accident.
5. She came downstairs when she had changed her clothes.
6. She was late because she had gotten lost.

9. **Aim: to review because and *after* + past perfect.**

Answers
1. Because he had eaten too much.
2. After she had paid the check.
3. After he had read the reviews.
4. After she had learned English.
5. Because he had forgotten the way.
6. After she had read it.

SOUNDS

1. **Aim: to focus on /w/ and /r/.**
● 📼 Some students may have problems pronouncing /w/ and /r/. Ask the students to say the words out loud. Then play the tape and ask them to repeat the words and put them in two columns.

Answers
/w/: world weeks wash water washing wear
/r/: return religion relative repair wrapping remind

2. **Aim: to focus on /ɔ:/ and /aʊ/.**
● These diphthongs can be difficult to pronounce. Ask the students to say the words and to put them in two groups.

● 📼 Play the tape and pause after each word. Ask the students to repeat the words.

Answers
/ɔ:/: poor door more roar soar bore pour four war
/aʊ/: power tower sour hour flower

● Point out that the same pronunciation can be represented by different spellings of the words.

3. **Aim: to focus on stress timing.**
● Remind the students that the stressed words in connected speech are the words which the speaker considers to be important. Ask the students to predict which words are likely to be stressed.

● 📼 Play the tape and ask the students to check their predictions.

Answers
<u>Suddenly</u>, someone <u>came up</u> from <u>behind</u>, <u>grabbed</u> my <u>bag</u> and <u>pulled</u> it <u>very hard</u>, <u>breaking</u> the <u>strap</u>. I <u>shouted</u>, first in <u>pain</u>, because when he <u>pulled</u> the bag it <u>hurt</u> my <u>wrist</u>, then in <u>anger</u> as I <u>saw</u> him <u>get</u> on a <u>motorcycle</u> and <u>drive away</u>.

4. **Aim: to practice writing.**
● Ask the students to write the important words on a separate piece of paper.

● They should turn to the instructions in the Communication Activity, and reconstitute the passage as accurately as possible from the important words.

SPEAKING

1. **Aim: to practice speaking and using the second conditional.**
● Ask the students to work in pairs and to discuss the situations in which they would do the things.

2. **Aim: to practice speaking.**
● Ask the students to work in groups and discuss their answers to activity 1. They should choose a situation which amuses, surprises, or shocks them and write a dialogue. Give them fifteen or twenty minutes, if possible, for this stage of the activity.

3. **Aim: to practice speaking.**
● Ask the groups in turn to act out their dialogues for the rest of the class.

Communication Activities

1. *Lesson 15*

Listening and Speaking, activity 1

Student B: 📼 Listen and put a check (✓) by Carlos's answers to these questions.

– What time does he have lunch and dinner?
  - ☐ noon and 6 P.M.
  - ☐ 12:30 P.M. and 6 P.M.
  - ☐ 1 P.M. and 7 P.M.

– Does he use a napkin? If so, where does he put it?
  - ☐ tucked under his chin
  - ☐ tied around his neck
  - ☐ on his lap or next to his plate

– Where does he put his hands when he's at the table but not eating?
  - ☐ on the table
  - ☐ he puts his elbows on the table
  - ☐ on his lap

When the recording stops, turn back to page 39.

2. *Lesson 3*

Vocabulary and Listening, activity 3

Group A: 📼 Listen to Barry and find the answers to these questions.

1. When is Australia Day?
2. What does the Melbourne Cup celebrate?
3. In what month is the Melbourne Cup?
4. What do people do before the race?
5. Who takes the day off?

When the recording stops, check that you all have the same answers. Then turn back to page 6.

3. *Lesson 15*

Listening and Speaking, activity 1

Student A: 📼 Listen and put a check (✓) by Carlos's answers to these questions.

– What does he say at the start of a meal?
  - ☐ "Enjoy your meal!"
  - ☐ "Cheers!"
  - ☐ nothing

– Does he usually use a knife and fork? If so, which hands does he hold them in?
  - ☐ fork in the left hand, knife in the right
  - ☐ he cuts with the fork in his left hand and the knife in his right, then puts the fork in his right hand to eat
  - ☐ he doesn't use a knife, he holds the fork in his left hand

– What food does he often eat with his hands at the table?
  - ☐ chicken ☐ pizza ☐ cheese ☐ cake
  - ☐ hamburgers ☐ fruit ☐ pie
  - ☐ sandwiches ☐ fries

– What does he say when someone raises their glass and makes a toast?
  - ☐ "Cheers!"
  - ☐ "Well said!"
  - ☐ nothing

When the recording stops, turn back to page 39.

4. *Progress Check 16–20*

Sounds, activity 4

Without looking at the passage, write it out in full. Use the stressed words to help you.

Now look back at the passage and check your version.

5. *Lesson 15*

Listening and Speaking, activity 1

Student C: 📼 Listen and put a check (✓) by Carlos's answers to these questions.

– How long does a typical lunch or dinner last?
  - ☐ 15 minutes ☐ 30 minutes ☐ 45 minutes

– Where does he put his knife and fork when he has finished a meal?
  - ☐ together in the center of the plate
  - ☐ together on the plate, slightly sideways
  - ☐ together on the plate in a V-shape

– When can he smoke during a meal?
  - ☐ before, during, and after
  - ☐ before and after
  - ☐ never

When the recording stops, turn back to page 39.

6. *Lesson 20*

Speaking and Writing, activity 2

Suddenly, high mountains sprang up around the chief's house. The chief and his men tried to climb the mountains, but they were too steep. Eventually they gave up and returned to live in their narrow valley.

Meanwhile, on the other side of the mountains, Wa and the villagers lived happily ever after, protected by the wonderful pearl.

7. *Lesson 3*

Vocabulary and Listening, activity 3

Group B: 🔲 Listen to Barry and find the answers to these questions.

1. What does Australia Day celebrate?
2. On what day of the week is the Melbourne Cup and at what time of day?
3. What year did the race start?
4. How long does it last?
5. Who is interested in the race?

When the recording stops, check that you all have the same answers. Then turn back to page 6.

Grammar Review

CONTENTS

Present simple

Form

You use the contracted form in spoken and informal written English.

Be

Affirmative		Negative	
I'm (I am)		I'm not (am not)	
you		you	
we	're (are)	we	aren't (are not)
they		they	
he		he	
she	's (is)	she	isn't (is not)
it		it	

Questions	Short answers
Am I	Yes, I am. No, I'm not.
Are you/we/they?	Yes, you/we/they are.
	No, you/we/they're not.
Is he/she/it?	Yes, he/she/it is.
	No, he/she/it isn't.

Have

Affirmative		Negative	
I		I	
you	have	you	haven't (have not)
we		we	
they		they	
he		he	
she	has	she	hasn't (has not)
it		it	

Questions	Short answers
Have I/you/we/they?	Yes, I/you/we/they have.
	No, I/you/we/they haven't.
Has he/she/it?	Yes, he/she/it has.
	No, he/she/it hasn't.

Regular verbs

Affirmative		Negative	
I		I	
you	work	you	don't (do not) work
we		we	
they		they	
he		he	
she	works	she	doesn't (does not) work
it		it	

Questions	Short answers
Do I/you/we/they work?	Yes, I/you/we/they do.
	No, I/you/we/they don't.
Does he/she/it work?	Yes, he/she/it does.
	No, he/she/it doesn't.

Question words with *is/are*

What's your name? Where are your parents?

Question words with *does/do*

What do you do? Where does he live?

Present simple: third person singular

(See Book A, Lesson 2.)

You add *-s* to most verbs.

takes, gets

You add *-es* to *do, go,* and verbs ending in *-ch, -ss-, -sh,* and

goes, does, watches, finishes

You add *-ies* to verbs ending in *-y*.

carries, tries

Use

You use the present simple:

● to talk about customs and habits. (See Book A, Lesson 1.)
   In my country men go to restaurants on their own.
● to talk about routine activities. (See Book A, Lesson 2.)
   He gets up at 6:30.
● to talk about a habit. (See Book A, Lesson 5.)
   He smokes twenty cigarettes a day.
● to talk about a personal characteristic. (See Book A, Lesson 5.)
   She plays the piano.
● to talk about a general truth. (See Book A, Lesson 5.)
   You change money in a bank.

Present continuous

Form

You form the present continuous with *be* + present participle *(-ing)*. You use the contracted form in spoken and informal written English.

Affirmative	Negative
I'm (am) working	I'm not (am not) working
you	you
we 're (are) working	we aren't (are not) working
they	they
he	he
she 's (is) working	she isn't (is not) working
it	it

Questions	Short answers
Am I working?	Yes, I am. No, I'm not.
Are you/we/they working?	Yes, you/we/they are.
	No, you/we/they aren't.
Is he/she/it working?	Yes, he/she/it is.
	No, he/she/it isn't.

Question words

What are you doing? Why are you laughing?

Present participle *(-ing)* endings

You form the present participle of most verbs by adding *-ing*.

go – going, visit – visiting

You add *-ing* to verbs ending in *-e*.

make – making, have – having

You double the final consonant of verbs of one syllable ending in a vowel and a consonant, and add *-ing*.

get- getting, shop- shopping

You add *-ing* to verbs ending in a vowel and *-y* or *-w*.

draw – drawing, play – playing

You don't usually use these verbs in the continuous form.

believe feel hear know like see smell sound taste think understand want

Use

You use the present continuous to say what is happening now or around now. There is an idea that the action or state is temporary. (See Book A, Lesson 5.)

It's raining. I'm learning English.

Past simple

Form

You use the contracted form in spoken and informal written English.

Be

Affirmative		Negative	
I		I	
he	was	he	wasn't (was not)
she		she	
it		it	
you		you	
we	were	we	weren't (were not)
they		they	

Have

Affirmative		Negative	
I		I	
you		you	
we		we	
they	had	they	didn't (did not) have
he		he	
she		she	
it		it	

Regular verbs

Affirmative		Negative	
I		I	
you		you	
we		we	
they	worked	they	didn't work
he		he	
she		she	
it		it	

Questions	Short answers
Did I/you/we/they work?	Yes, I/you/we/they did.
he/she/it	he/she/it
	No, I/you/we/they didn't.
	he/she/it

Question words

What did you do? Why did you leave?

Past simple endings

You add *-ed* to most regular verbs.
walk – walked, watch – watched
You add *-d* to verbs ending in *-e*.
close – closed, continue – continued
You double the consonant and add *-ed* to verbs ending in a vowel and a consonant.
stop – stopped, plan – planned
You drop the *-y* and add *-ied* to verbs ending in *-y*.
study – studied, try – tried
You add *-ed* to verbs ending in a vowel + *-y*.
play – played, annoy – annoyed

Pronunciation of past simple endings

/t/ *finished, liked, walked*
/d/ *continued, lived, stayed*
/ɪd/ *decided, started, visited*

Expressions of past time

(See Book A, Lesson 8.)
yesterday   the day before yesterday   last weekend
  last night   last month   last year

Use

You use the past simple:
- to talk about a past action or event that is finished. (See Book A, Lessons 6, 7, and 8.)
  He shipped it over from the River Thames.

Future simple (*will*)

Form

You form the future simple with *will* + infinitive. You use the contracted form in spoken and informal written English.

Affirmative		Negative	
I		I	
you		you	
we		we	
they	'll (will) work	they	won't (will not) work
he		he	
she		she	
it		it	

Questions	Short answers
Will I/you/we/they work?	Yes, I/you/we/they will.
he/she/it/	he/she/it/
	No, I/you/we/they won't.
	he/she/it/

Question words

What will you do? Where will you go?

Expressions of future time

tomorrow   tomorrow morning   tomorrow afternoon
next week   next month   next year   in two days
in three months   in five years

Use

You use the future simple:
- to make a prediction or express an opinion about the future. (See Book A, Lesson 12.)
  I think most people will need English for their jobs.
- to talk about decisions you make at the moment of speaking. (See Book A, Lesson 13.)
  I'll give you the money right now.
- to talk about things you are not sure will happen with *probably* and *perhaps*. (See Book A, Lesson 13.)
  He'll probably spend three weeks there. Perhaps he'll stay two days in Rio.
- to offer to do something. (See Book A, Lesson 13 and Book B, Lesson 10.)
  OK, I'll buy some food.

Present perfect simple

Form

You form the present perfect with *has/have* + past participle. You use the contracted form in spoken and informal written English.

Affirmative		Negative	
I		I	
you	've (have) worked	you	haven't (have not) worked
we		we	
they		they	
he		he	
she	's (has) worked	she	hasn't (has not) worked
it		it	

Questions	Short answers
Have I/you/we/they worked?	Yes, I/you/we/they have.
	No, I/you/we/they haven't.
Has he/she/it worked?	Yes, he/she/it has.
	No, he/she/it hasn't.

Past participles

All regular and some irregular verbs have past participles which are the same as their past simple form.
Regular: *move – moved, finish – finished, visit – visited*
Irregular: *leave – left, find – found, buy – bought*
Some irregular verbs have past participles which are not the same as the past simple form.
go – went – gone, be – was/were – been, drink – drank – drunk, ring – rang – rung

Been and *gone*

He's been to Canada = He's been there and he's back here now.
He's gone to Canada = He's still there.

Use

You use the present perfect:
- to talk about past experiences. You often use it with *ever* and *never*. (See Book B, Lesson 1.)
  Have you ever stayed in the hospital?
  I've had food poisoning several times.
  I've never broken my leg.
- to talk about a past action which has a result in the present. It is not important when the action happened. You often use it to describe changes. (See Book B, Lesson 2.)
  She's gotten married.
  I've moved to a new house.
  Have you found a new job?

You often use just to emphasize that something has happened very recently.
She's just had a baby.
- to talk about an action or state which began in the past and continues to the present. You use *for* to talk about the length of time. (See Book B, Lesson 3.)
  I've been here for two hours.
  You use *since* to say when the action or state began.
  I've been here since 8 o'clock.

8 o'clock	Now—10 o'clock
I arrived.	*I am still here.*

Remember that if you ask for and give more information about these experiences, actions, or states such as *when, how, why,* and *how long,* you use the past simple.
When did you stay in the hospital? In 1996.
How long did you stay there? A week.

Past continuous

Form

You form the past continuous with *was/were* + present participle. You use the contracted form in spoken and informal written English.

Affirmative		Negative	
I		I	
he	was working	he	wasn't (was not) working
she		she	
it		it	
you		you	
we	were working	we	weren't (were not) working
they		they	

Questions	Short answers
Was I/he/she/it working	Yes, I/he/she/it was.
	No, I/he/she/it wasn't.
Were you/we/they working?	Yes, you/we/they were.
	No, you/we/they weren't.

You don't usually use these verbs in the continuous form.
believe feel hear know like see smell sound taste think understand want

Use

You use the past continuous:
- to talk about something that was in progress at a specific time in the past. (See Book B, Lesson 11.)
  What were you doing at nine o'clock yesterday morning? I was going to work.

8:30 A.M.	9 A.M.	9:30 A.M.
I left home.		*I arrived at work.*

- to talk about something that was in progress at the time something else happened or interrupted it. You join the parts of the sentences with *when* and *while*. (See Book B, Lessons 11 and 12.)
They were driving along in silence when Francesca suddenly said, "There it is!"
The verb in the *while* clause is usually in the past continuous.
While I was walking home, I had a strange experience.
Remember that you use *when* + past simple to describe two things which happened one after the other.
When I got closer, I noticed a young couple sitting in the garden.

Past perfect

Form

You form the past perfect with *had* + past participle. You use the contracted form in spoken and informal written English.

Affirmative	Negative
I	I
you	you
we	we
they 'd(had) worked	they hadn't (had not) worked
he	he
she	she
it	it

Questions	Short answers
Had I/you/we/they worked?	Yes, I/you/we/they had.
he/she/it/	he/she/it/
	No, I/you/we/they hadn't.
	he/she/it/

Use

You use the past perfect:

- to talk about one past action that happened before another past action. You often use *after*, *when*, and *because*, and you use the past simple for the second action. (See Book B, Lesson 20.)
After she had cured the girl, she went back to her village.

Earlier past	Past	Now
She cured the girl.	*She went back to her village.*	

When she had cured the girl, she went back to her village.
Because she had fallen asleep, the chief's son was angry.

Verb patterns

There are several possible patterns after certain verbs which involve *-ing* form verbs and infinitive constructions with or without *to*.

-ing form verbs

You can put an *-ing* form verb after certain verbs. (See Book A, Lesson 4.)
I love walking. She likes swimming. They hate lying on the beach.
Remember that *would like to do something* refers to an activity at a specific time in the future.
I'd like to go to the movies next Saturday.
Try not to confuse it with *like doing something* which refers to an activity you enjoy all the time.
I like going to the movies. I go most weekends.

Use

You use an *-ing* form verb:
- to describe the purpose of something after *to be for*. (See Book B, Lesson 5.)
A cassette player is for playing cassettes.
- to ask people to do things after *would you mind*. (See Book B, Lesson 10.)
Would you mind lending it to me?

To + infinitive

You can put *to* + infinitive after many verbs. Here are some of them:
agree decide go have hope earn leave like need offer start try want

Use

You use *to* + infinitive:
- with *(be) going to* and *would like to*. (See below.)
- to describe the purpose of something. (See Book B, Lesson 5.)
You use a cassette player to play cassettes.

Have to

You use *have to* and *have got to* to talk about something you're obliged or strongly advised to do:
You have to wear a helmet.
In negatives, you use *don't have to*:
You don't have to go to work on Sunday.
Don't have to means that something is not necessary.

Going to

You use *(be) going to*:
- to talk about future intentions or plans. (See Book A, Lesson 11 and Book B, Lesson 5.)
I'm going to be a doctor. (I'm studying medicine.)
- to talk about things which are arranged and sure to happen with *(be) going to*. (See Book A, Lesson 13.)
I'm going to visit South America. I've bought my ticket.

You often use the present continuous and not *going to* with *come and go*.
Are you coming tonight?
NOT ~~Are you going to come tonight?~~
He's going to South America.
NOT ~~He's going to go to South America~~.

Would like to

You use *would like to*:
● to talk about ambitions, hopes, or preferences. (See Book A, Lesson 11.)
I'd like to speak English fluently.

Modal verbs

The following verbs are modal verbs.
an could may might must should will would

Form

Modal verbs:
● have the same form for all persons.
I can run a mile. She can speak five languages.
● don't take the auxiliary *do* in questions and negatives.
Can you drive? You must not lean out of the window.
● take an infinitive without *to*.
I can type. You should see a doctor.

Use

You use *can*:
● to express general ability, something you are able to do on most occasions. (See Book B, Lesson 7.)
I can run a mile.
● to say what you're allowed to do or what it is possible to do. (See Book B, Lesson 8.)
You can cross when the sign says "Walk."
to ask for permission. (See Book B, Lesson 10.)
Can I smoke?
● to ask people to do things. (See Book B, Lesson 10.)
Can you speak louder, please?
Can is a little less formal than *could*.
You use *can't*:
● to say what you're not allowed to do or what it is not possible to do. (See Book B, Lesson 8.)
You can't cross when the sign says "Don't walk."
You can also use *must not*.
You must not cross when the sign says "Don't walk."
You use *could*:
● to express general ability in the past. (See Book B, Lesson 7.)
When I was five, I could swim, but I couldn't write my own name.
● to ask for permission. (See Book B, Lesson 10.)
Could I leave now?

● to ask people to do things. (See Book B, Lesson 10.)
Could you help me?
Could is a little more formal than *can*.
You use *may*:
● to ask for permission. (See Book B, Lesson 10.)
May I call you Mary?
● to talk about possible future events. (See Book B, Lesson 16.)
It may rain tomorrow.
May has almost the same meaning as *might*.
You use *might*:
● to talk about possible future events. (See Book B, Lesson 16.)
It might rain tomorrow.
You don't usually use *might* in questions.
You use *must*:
● to talk about something you are obliged to do.
It's late. I must go now. You really must stop smoking.
You use *should*:
● to give advice. It can also express a mild obligation or the opinion of the speaker. (See Book B, Lesson 9.)
You should do some exercise. You shouldn't smoke.
● *Ought (not) to* has the same meaning as *should(n't)*.
You ought to do some exercise.
For the uses of *will* see *Future simple (will)*
You use *would*:
● to ask for permission with *mind if*. (See Book B, Lesson 10.)
Would you mind if I borrowed it?
● to ask people to do things with *mind* + *-ing* form verbs. (See Book B, Lesson 10.)
Would you mind lending it to me?
● to talk about the consequences of an imaginary situation. (See Book B, Lesson 18.)
I'd go to New York City.

Conditionals

First conditional

Form

You form the first conditional with *if* + present simple *will* + infinitive.
If you touch it, you'll get a shock.

Use

You use the first conditional to talk about a likely situation and to describe its result. You talk about the likely situation with *if* + present simple. You describe the result with *will* or *won't*. (See Book B, Lesson 17.)
If you give it to me, I'll let you go.
If it doesn't stop rising, we won't be able to escape.
You often use the contracted form in speech and informal writing. The *if* clause can come at the beginning or at the end of the sentence.

Second conditional

Form

You form the second conditional with *if* + past simple
would + infinitive.
If I found some money in the street, I'd take it to the police.
You can also use the past continuous in the *if* clause.
If it was raining, I'd take an umbrella.

Use

You use the second conditional to talk about an imaginary
or unlikely situation and its result. You talk about the
imaginary or unlikely situation with *if* + past tense. You
describe the result with *would or wouldn't*. (See Book B,
Lesson 19.)
If I won a free vacation, I would go to Bali.
If I had $1 million, I wouldn't have to work.
You often use the contracted form in speech and informal
writing. The *if* clause can come at the beginning or at the
end of the sentence. It is still common to see *were* and not
was in the *if* clause.
If I were taller, I'd play basketball.

Present simple passive

Form

You form the present simple passive with *am/is/are* + past
participle.
A feast is prepared.
Stores are filled with symbols of death.

Use

You use the passive to focus on the object of the sentence.
You can use it when you don't know who or what does
something. The object of an active sentence becomes the
subject of a passive sentence. (See Book B, Lesson 13.)
A bowl of water is placed on the table.
If you are more interested in the object, but you know who
or what does something, you use *by*.
A special kind of bread is baked by the men.

Have got

Form

You use the contracted form in spoken and informal
written English.

Affirmative		Negative	
I		I	
you	've (have) got	you	haven't (have not) got
we		we	
they		they	
he		he	
she	's (has) got	she	hasn't (has not) got
it		it	

Questions	Short answers
Have I/you/we/they got?	Yes, I/you/we/they have
	No, I/you/we/they haven't.
Has he/she/it got?	Yes, he/she/it has.
	No, he/she/it hasn't.

Use

You use *have got* to talk about facilities, possession, or
relationship. (See Book A, Lesson 10.)
I've got a new car.
You don't use *have got* to talk about a habit or routine.
I often have lunch out. NOT I often have got lunch out.
You don't usually use *have got* in the past. You use the past
simple of *have*.
I had a headache yesterday. NOT I had got a headache.

Questions

You can form questions in two ways:
- with a question word such as *who, what, which, where, how, why*.
  What's your name?
- without a question word.
  Are you American?

You can put a noun after *what* and *which*. (See Book A,
Lesson 1.)
What time is it? Which road will you take?
You often say *what* to give the idea that there is more
choice.
What books have you read lately?
You can put an adjective or an adverb after *how*. (See Book
A, Lessons 15 and 20.)
*How much is it? How long does it take by car? How fast
can you drive?*
You can use *who, what,* or *which* as pronouns to ask about
the subject of the sentence. You don t use *do* or *did*. (See
Book A, Lessons 1 and 7.)
What's your first name?
Who invented the first traveler's check?
You can use *who, what,* or *which* and other question
words to ask about the object of the sentence. You use *do*
or *did*. (See Book A, Lessons 1 and 7.)
What did he call his invention?

Restrictive relative clauses

- You use a restrictive relative clause to define people,
  things, and places. The information in the restrictive
  relative clause is important for the sense of the sentence.
  (See Book B, Lesson 4.)
You use *who* for people.
A journalist is someone who writes for a newspaper.

You use *which* for things.
A subway is a railroad which runs under the ground.
You often use *that* instead of *who* or *which*.
A journalist is someone that writes for a newspaper.
A subway is a railroad that runs under the ground.
You use *where* for places.
A parking lot is a place where you park your car.
You use *that* after a superlative adjective instead of *who,*
which, or *where*. (See Book A, Lesson 19.)
Who is the nicest person that you know?
What is the most expensive thing that you own?
Remember that there is no comma before a restrictive
relative clause. In speech there is no pause.

Articles

You can find the main uses of articles in Book A, Lesson 3.
Here are some extra details.
You use *an* for nouns which begin with a vowel.
an armchair
You use *one* if you want to emphasize the number.
One hundred and twenty-two.
Before vowels you pronounce *the* /ðiː/.
You do not use the definite article with parts of the body.
You use a possessive adjective.
I'm washing my hair.

Plurals

You can find the main rules for forming plurals in Book A,
Lesson 3.

Possessives

You can find the main uses of the possessive *'s* in Book A,
Lesson 9. You can find a list of possessive adjectives in
Book A, Lesson 9.

Expressions of quantity

Countable and uncountable nouns

Countable nouns have both a singular and a plural form.
(See Book A, Lesson 15.)
an apple – some apples, a melon – some melons,
a potato – some potatoes, a cup – (not) many cups,
a cookie – a few cookies
Uncountable nouns do not usually have a plural form.
some wine, some cheese, some fruit, (not) much meat, a
little coffee
If you talk about different kinds of uncountable nouns they
become countable.
Beaujolais and Bordeaux are both French wines.

Expressions with countable or uncountable nouns

You can put countable or uncountable nouns with these
expressions of quantity.
lots of apples, lots of cheese, hardly any apples, hardly any
cheese, a lot of fruit, a lot of potatoes.

Some and *any*

(See Book A, Lesson 15.)

Affirmative *There's some milk in the refrigerator.*
There are some apples on the table.
Negative *I haven't got any brothers.*
There isn't any cheese.

Questions
You usually use *any* for questions.
Is there any sugar?
You can use *some* in questions when you are making an
offer or a request, and you expect the answer to be *yes*.
Would you like some coffee?
Can I have some sugar, please?

Much and *many*

You use *many* with countable nouns and *much* with
uncountable nouns. (See Book A, Lesson 15.)
How many eggs would you like?
How much butter do you need?

Too much/many, not enough, fewer, less, and more

You can put a countable noun in the plural after *too many,*
not enough, and *fewer.*
There are too many people.
There aren't enough clean rivers.
In the United States there are fewer men than women.
You can put an uncountable noun after *too much, not*
enough, more, and *less.*
There's too much noise. There isn't enough farmland.
There's more pollution.
You can put an adjective after *too* or between *not* and
enough.
The sea is too polluted. The air isn't clean enough.

Making comparisons

Comparative and superlative adjectives

Form
You add *-er* to most adjectives for the comparative form,
and *-est* for the superlative form. (See Book A, Lesson 18.)
cold colder coldest   cheap cheaper cheapest
You add *-r* to adjectives ending in *-e* for the comparative
form and *-st* for the superlative form.
large larger largest   fine finer finest

You add *-ier* to adjectives ending in *-y* for the comparative form, and *-iest* for the superlative form.

happy happier happiest
friendly friendlier friendliest

You double the last letter of adjectives ending in *-g, -t,* or *-n.*

hot hotter hottest
thin thinner thinnest

You use *more* for the comparative form and *most* for the superlative form of longer adjectives.

expensive more expensive most expensive
important more important most important

Some adjectives have irregular comparative and superlative forms.

good better best   bad worse worst

More than, less than, as ... as

- You put *than* before the object of comparison. (See Book A, Lesson 19.)
  Children wear more casual clothes than their parents.
- You use *less ... than* to change the focus of the comparison.
  Parents wear less casual clothes than their children.
- You can put *much* before the comparative adjective, *more,* or *less* to emphasize it.
  They're much less formal than they were.
- You use *as ... as* to show something is the same.
  They're as casual as teenagers all over the world.
- You use *not as ... as* to show something is different.
  Dresses are not as popular as in Western countries.

But, however, although

You use *but, however,* and *although* to make a comparison which focuses on a difference. (See Book B, Lesson 15.)
You use *but* to join two sentences. You don't usually use *but* at the beginning of a sentence.
We drink coffee in the morning, but we don't drink it in the afternoon.
You use *although* at the beginning of a subordinate clause. You need to separate the subordinate and the main clause with a comma.
We usually have dinner at six, although some people have dinner later.
You can put the subordinate clause at the beginning or at the end of the sentence.
Although we usually have dinner at six, some people have dinner later.
You put *however* at the beginning of a sentence. You put a comma after it.
We drink coffee in the morning. However, we don't drink it in the afternoon.

So, because

- You can join two sentences with *so* to describe a consequence.
  She often took the plane so she didn't look at the safety instructions.
- You can join the same two sentences with *because* to describe a reason.
  She didn't look at the safety instructions because she often took the plane.

Prepositions of place

(See Book A, Lesson 14.)

Prepositions of time and place: *in, at, on, to*

Use
You use *in*:
- with times of the day: *in the morning, in the afternoon.*
- with months of the year: *in March, in September*
- with years: *in 1996, in 1872*
- with places: *in New York, in Mexico City, in the bank*

You use *at*:
- with times of the day: *at night, at seven o'clock*
- with places: *at the theater, at the stadium*

You use *on*:
- with days, dates: *on Friday, on July 15th*

You use *to*:
- with places: *Let's go to Seattle.*

Adverbs of frequency

Use
You use an adverb of frequency to say how often things happen. (See Book A, Lesson 1.)
They always take their shoes off.
We usually take wine or flowers.
We often wear jeans and sweaters.
We sometimes arrive about fifteen minutes after.
We never ask personal questions.

Tapescripts

Lesson 2 Listening, activity 1

DIANE October 10, 1995: I just can't believe it! After seven years working there, Chuck has lost his job at the car factory. They're going to close the factory because they've decided to move it to a foreign country. It's so unfair. What are we going to do?

December 27, 1995: What a sad Christmas! Only one present each under the tree. I wanted so much to get new clothes for Ben. And Chuck is really depressed. He's tried so hard to find another job, but he's had no luck. It's the wrong time of the year, I guess.

January 22, 1996: Ben has just turned two. He's growing up so fast! We celebrated his birthday with pizza and a chocolate cake, but we couldn't afford any nice presents. If Chuck doesn't find work pretty soon, I might start looking for a job myself, but I'm not qualified for anything...

February 14, 1996: I've found a job! I start on Monday. I'm going to work as a saleswoman in a department store. They said I didn't need any qualifications, because they would train me on the job. Chuck is going to stay home and take care of Ben, but he's not too happy about it... He thinks he's going to be bored! Somehow I don't think he will be!

February 19, 1996: I've just finished my first day at work. It was fun and the people were really kind and helpful. But I'm exhausted, Ben is screaming, and Chuck is complaining that he has too much housework to do—and he hasn't even made dinner yet!

July 4, 1996: Chuck and Ben have become so close—I think I'm a little bit jealous of Chuck, but I'm really enjoying my job. And I really think Chuck likes being at home now. He's keeping the house much cleaner, and his cooking is getting a little better.

October 28, 1996: I've just been promoted. The manager said I am one of the best workers she has! This means more pay—but also longer hours! I really miss Ben and Chuck when I'm at work.

January 21, 1997: I can't believe it... Ben is going to be three tomorrow! So much has happened in the past year. We've bought him a great train set—but I think Chuck is more excited to play with it than Ben!

Lesson 3 Vocabulary and Listening, activity 3

Q Are there any, you know, um... special days or events that everyone in Australia celebrates?

BARRY Well, there's Christmas and Easter, like you have in the States, I mean. They're pretty important.

Q I was thinking more of national holidays, like Independence Day or events that happen in your town or region, you know, local festivals or something like that. I don't even know if you have an Independence Day in Australia.

BARRY Well, that's because we're not really independent, are we? At least, not yet. But I suppose there's Australia Day, which we celebrate on... the 26th of January.

Q Oh, and what does that celebrate?

BARRY It's the day Captain Cook arrived in Botany Bay in Sydney in 1788, bringing Europeans to Australia. But the trouble is, we don't really celebrate it very much usually, except on special anniversaries, like in 1988 which was 200 years after he arrived. Um... no, there's one day which people really enjoy and that's the Melbourne Cup in November.

Q Oh, and what does the Melbourne Cup celebrate?

BARRY It's a horse race.

Q A horse race?

BARRY Yeah, the whole country stops during the horse race, and everyone wants to know which horse wins. We love horse racing.

Q And, uh... you say it takes place in November?

BARRY Yeah, the first, um... the first Tuesday in November. At two-forty in the afternoon, every year.

Q And when did it first take place?

BARRY I think it started in 1874.

Q And what exactly happens?

BARRY Well, people from all over Australia come to Melbourne on special planes and trains for the day and dress up and go to Flemington race course. And they take picnics in their cars which they eat before the race. Um… and everyone bets on the horse they think is going to win. And then the race starts.

Q At exactly two forty?

BARRY That's right. And at two forty-three, it's all over.

Q So, it only takes three minutes?

BARRY Yes, and if you're enjoying yourself too much, you miss it. It's great fun and a great social occasion, a kind of, um… social ritual at the start of summer.

Q Is it a public holiday?

BARRY It is in the city of Melbourne and the whole of the State of Victoria. Everybody takes the day off. But not in the rest of Australia.

Q But even people who can't go to Melbourne are interested in the race?

BARRY Oh, yeah. The interesting thing is that the whole of Australia wants to know who wins the Melbourne Cup. Everybody listens to the race on the radio or watches it on television. The traffic stops and in Canberra, the politicians stop work in parliament.

Q Wow! So everyone's involved, even people outside Melbourne.

BARRY That's right. It's a kind of state occasion for the whole of Australia.

Lesson 4 Vocabulary and Listening, activity 2

A Um… "trousers" are… an item of clothing. Yes?

B Oh, I know what trousers are! Yes… we call them "pants."

A Oh, right.

B Oh, the snack food that's round and flat and fried and thin and very crisp, we call them, um… "chips… potato chips."

A Oh, right. Um… cold, you mean? Yes, we call those, um… "crisps". You buy them in a packet… "crisps."

B Um… if I need some medicine or something like that, I go to a "drugstore."

A Right, we call that a "chemist." Um… a "state school" is a school which is funded by the state, it's the opposite of a private school, in other words.

B Oh yes, we call that "public school."

A Oh, right.

B OK. When you need to cross the street, you use the "crosswalk."

A Ah yes, we call that a "zebra crossing."

B A what?

A A "zebra crossing"… you know, 'cause it's striped, like a zebra.

B Oh, I see, "zebra!" That's so cute!

A Yes, I suppose it is…

B Um… when I get a hamburger I also like to get "french fries," which are the strips of, um… fried potato.

A Oh, right—"chips" we call those.

B Do you?

A Yes, "chips." Um… when you travel around, for example in London on… on the train under the ground, that's called the "underground."

B No…

A Yes.

B It's called a "subway."

A No. The "underground," yes…

B Well, that's what we call it. Every town in the States has a "main street" where all the shops and things are.

A Oh, right … No, we call that the "high street". Same thing, "high street."

Lesson 5 **Listening, activity 2**

SPEAKER 1 Well, it's... it's that stuff you need to put two different pieces together. For instance, two pieces of paper. You put that stuff on one bit of paper and stick the other paper on top of it, for example. Or, you can do that with leather too, if your shoe gets broken, or you can do that with wood, and things like that.

SPEAKER 2 It's a piece of material. Um... it's like a rectangle and it's soft and you use it to... after a bath for drying yourself when you're wet.

SPEAKER 3 It looks like little pieces of wood, very thin little pieces all in a box and, um... at the tip there's a... well, they're either black or red and it's something you use to light a fire or anything like that.

SPEAKER 4 Um... I want... you put it on when it's hot and you buy it in a bottle, a plastic bottle and you put it on your body and it protects you from the sun.

SPEAKER 5 It's a machine for cleaning. You have a tube and it, um... it sucks the dust. It's a machine for cleaning the carpet or the floor.

Fluency 1 **Listening and Speaking, activity 6**

Q Tell me, Gary, is it true that in the United States you never speak to people you don't know? What about your neighbors? Do you talk to them? Does it depend on whether you know them well or not?

GARY Well, neighbors are different. They're a little bit too close, and maybe it's just safer not to talk to them.

Q OK. How about when you greet people, people you know. Do you kiss them?

GARY Well, some people I know do, but I generally don't. No, I don't feel comfortable kissing my friends.

Q I think people are often surprised by the way Americans use people's first names a lot. What do you think is the rule for this? For example, do you think we use first names as soon as we meet people for the first time? Or do we wait until we get to know them a little better?

GARY Well, I think you're right—in America we do tend to be friendly and um, yeah, if I meet someone for the first time, depending on the situation, I will use their first name.

Q Hmm. OK. I've another question. Do you think Americans smile when they're embarrassed or when we don't want to hurt someone's feelings?

GARY Smile? Um. No, I don't think so. I think we pretty much show our feelings, just how we're feeling it.

Q OK. Now, would you say that American men stand up when a woman enters the room? Or is that old-fashioned now?

GARY It depends how old you are. Um...

Q Fair enough. Well, what about when a man and a woman are both entering room. Does the man still let the woman go into the room first?

GARY I do. I want her to see what's going on before I come in.

Q OK. Now suppose you're out shopping. Do you say hello and goodbye to store clerks?

GARY No, no, not unless I shop there a lot. No, I don't do that.

Q OK. Now is there a difference between what you would do in a small store and a large store?

GARY Well, if it's a small store, maybe a little more friendly, I—I might say hello and goodbye, even have a short conversation. In a big store, it's a little colder, and um, you just go in, get what you want and leave.

Q OK. Well, Gary thank you very much.

Lesson 6 **Vocabulary and Listening, activity 3**

Conversation 1

POLICE OFFICER May I see your driver's license and vehicle registration, sir?

DRIVER Uhh... sure... uh... here's my driver's license, and... Oh darn! I must have left the registration at home!

PASSENGER No you didn't! You don't have a registration...

DRIVER Sshh!

POLICE OFFICER And I'll need to see proof of insurance, please sir.

DRIVER Oh, that's in the other car...

PASSENGER You don't have another car!

DRIVER Keep quiet, will you!

POLICE OFFICER Do you know what the speed limit is here, sir?

DRIVER Uh... 70?

POLICE OFFICER No, sir, it's 55. You were doing 110 mph, sir. You have to slow down a bit...

DRIVER Yeah, right, well, uh... my wife is very sick and she's got to get to a hospital right now, so if you could just let us go...

PASSENGER I am NOT sick!

DRIVER SSSHHH!

POLICE OFFICER Well, sir, I'm afraid I have to write a ticket for this... and the fine is going to be about $800.

DRIVER Oh, I can't afford that! You see, I have to look after my sick brother. He's in a wheelchair...

PASSENGER You don't even have a brother!

DRIVER Oh, shut up, Debbie!

POLICE OFFICER Is he always this rude to you, ma'am?

PASSENGER No, only when he's drunk...

Conversation 2

BUS DRIVER I'm sorry, lady, you can't bring that dog on the bus.

PASSENGER Why not? I'll pay for him.

BUS DRIVER Transit Authority rules, ma'am. No dogs.

PASSENGER But that man has a dog. You have to tell him to get off, too.

BUS DRIVER That's a seeing eye dog, ma'am. The gentleman is blind.

PASSENGER Oh... well, why don't you let other dogs on? I think it's absurd... I can't walk downtown. It's too far!

BUS DRIVER Hey, I don't make the rules—I just have to follow them.

PASSENGER Well can't you make an exception, just this time?

BUS DRIVER Sorry, no. Now please move aside and let the other passengers on the bus.

PASSENGER Well, this is an outrage! I'm going to write to the mayor...

Conversation 3

AIRPORT STAFF Excuse me, sir, is this your bag?

PASSENGER Umm... yeah, it is.

AIRPORT STAFF I have to ask you some security questions... Did you pack the bag?

PASSENGER Uh-huh.

AIRPORT STAFF And has it left your sight since you packed it?

PASSENGER Umm... no, I guess not.

AIRPORT STAFF Did anyone give you a package or anything to take with you on this trip, sir?

PASSENGER No.

AIRPORT STAFF And do you have any battery-operated equipment in your bag, sir?

PASSENGER Well, I have my laptop, and a Walkman...

AIRPORT STAFF I'm afraid we have to remove the batteries, sir. Please open the bag.

PASSENGER Uh... OK.

Lesson 7 **Listening and Speaking, activity 2**

The Skylight, part 1

The heat, as the cab drove up the hill, became more violent. The woman sat in the back of the car with a five-year-old boy beside her, his thumb in his mouth.

"Are we there yet?" the boy asked.

"Soon."

The child's eyes closed. "Oh no," she thought. "He can't go to sleep yet." She could hear herself telling the story in the cold Vermont spring. "It makes so much sense to take this house for the summer. It's in the mountains, two hours' drive from Mexico City. I'll go first with Johnny, and Phil will bring the girls when school gets out. And the Garcias will have everything ready for us." But now it was real. She was hot and afraid. Will everything be all right when we get there, she wondered. Suddenly, the driver turned off the road, drove up a narrow track, and stopped. The woman could only see stones and grass.

"But—where?"

He pointed and got out. He picked up their suitcases and walked away. She took the child's hand and followed the driver. Above them, on the terrace, was the square grey house. A small skylight in the roof caught the sun. The shutters and doors were all closed.

"You have the key, ma'am?"

"The key? But Mr. and Mrs. Garcia are expecting us."

The driver tried the door. It was locked. She knocked. There was no answer.

Lesson 7   **Listening and Speaking, activity 4**

The Skylight, part 2

The driver wanted his money. She paid him and he disappeared. She heard the cab leaving.

"Why can't we go into the house?" asked Johnny.

"Because it's locked."

She looked up and saw the skylight.

"If there was a ladder, maybe we could..."

"There's a ladder," he said. "Can we lift it?"

It was quite light.

"Are you going to climb up there?" the child asked.

She hesitated. "Yes, I guess so."

She started to climb. At the top she saw the tiny skylight was open. She couldn't get through it, but a child could do it. She could lower Johnny through, and he could run downstairs and unlock a window. She came down the ladder. He was lying on the ground, nearly asleep.

"Johnny," she said. "Would you like to climb the ladder?"

"Right now? Can I really?"

"Yes, yes you can. When you've gotten through the skylight, I want you to do something." She explained, very carefully.

Together they climbed the ladder. She lowered him through the window until he stood on a table.

"Can you get down?" she asked.

"Yes. Shall I go and open the window now?"

"Yes," she said. "And hurry."

She climbed down the ladder, went to the window and waited. It was getting dark.

"Johnny, it's this one. Are you there, Johnny?"

Give him time, she thought. He's only five. He can't hurry. She climbed up the ladder again and shouted, "Johnny, can you hear me?" Her voice had no volume, no echo.

Lesson 7   **Listening and Speaking, activity 6**

The Skylight, part 3

It was now dark. She went down again and ran around the house, shouting his name. Something has happened to him. I must go for help. She ran to the road and when she saw the lights of the car, she waved her arms to stop it. She started to cry. It was a long time before the three men understood.

"But how can we get in? We have no tools," they said.

"There's a farm back there. Will you take me?" They let her into the car.

"Turn around. It's back there on the left. There it is!"

They turned off the road. She got out of the car and ran to the front door. A small woman in pants opened the door.

"My dear, what's happened?"

"You speak English?" She told her the story. Another woman appeared.

"Maria," Miss Jardine said, "Get some tools, a hammer and an ax."

They all got into the car and went back to the house. They drove up the lane and stopped. She ran to the house, calling, "Johnny! Johnny!"

Lesson 7   **Listening and Speaking, activity 8**

The Skylight, part 4

One of the men took an ax and smashed the shutters. She was quickly through the window.

"Johnny, where are you?"

She ran up the stairs. A door on the first floor was open. He was lying on the floor, fast asleep. Surrounding him were lots of toys. She shook him gently. He opened his eyes.

"I like the toys," he said.

His thumb went back into his mouth and his eyes closed again. She sat with her head on her knees, her arms around her body.

"Oh, thank God, " she whispered. "Thank God."

Lesson 8   **Listening, activity 1**

Q   OK, Jane, um... Let's say you're waiting to cross the street, and the sign says "Don't Walk" but there are no cars coming. Can you cross?

JANE Sure!

Q   But what if a police officer sees you?

JANE Umm... well I guess that all depends on the mood of the cop. She might give you a ticket...

Q   Really?

JANE Yeah, I mean, technically jay walking—crossing the street when the light tells you not to—is against the law... but I bet the average American would do it anyway!

Q   I see... what about if you are in a park on a hot summer's day, and you're having a picnic. Can you drink beer?

JANE Well, technically not!

Q   No? Why not?

JANE Well, 'cause if you get caught, there's a $100 fine!

Q   Right, OK! Well how about if you're with some young children, and you want to go into a bar. Can the kids go with you?

JANE Well... They can't go into a place that's strictly a bar—you have to be 21 for that—but if it's a restaurant that has a part of it that's a bar... they can go into the restaurant part.

Q   Right... Now, what about smoking... You're flying from New York to Washington D.C. Can you smoke a cigarette?

JANE No, thank God!

Q   Why is that?

JANE Oh, I can't stand it when people smoke on planes! No, you can't smoke on *any* domestic flights now. I wish they'd do that on international flights, too!

Q   Yeah, right, it is kind of smelly...

JANE And it makes your eyes sting and... ugh!

Q   OK, now... Imagine a friend gives you a sweater for your birthday. You've worn it a couple of times, but you decide that you don't really like it... it doesn't suit you, or whatever. Can you take it back to the store to get a refund or to exchange it for something else?

JANE Well, you can, depending on where you bought it. Some places will ask for a receipt, and won't take it back if it looks like you've worn it. But other stores have a policy where they'll take anything back, no matter what.

Q   Even without a receipt?

JANE Even without a receipt! This is America!

Q   Right! OK, last question...

JANE Hmm?

Q   You're in a large bookstore, but you don't have much money—so you aren't going to buy anything. Can you sit and read the books and magazines?

JANE Well, sure, why not?

Q   So no one would hassle you... ask you to leave the store?

JANE No! I mean, if you were there all day, they might get suspicious. And I'm sure they won't let homeless people do that... but... you know...

Q   But they wouldn't mind if you did it?

JANE No... actually, I do it all the time!

Lesson 9   **Listening, activity 2**

Q   So, Doctor Samuels, what do you advise for people who want to avoid jet lag?

DOCTOR The thing about flying is that it has a dehydrating effect on the body, and this means that you need to replace the missing liquid with a lot of water. It's also better to avoid alcohol, as this only makes the dehydrating effect worse. So, plenty of water or juice, and adjust your body clock by adopting the time of your destination as soon as possible. So even if your body tells you it's time for bed, try to stay awake until it's bedtime in your new time zone.

Q   And what can you do to avoid an upset stomach?

DOCTOR Mmm. One of the main causes of an upset stomach when you're in a foreign country is the water supply. So, the most important thing to do is to drink only bottled or boiled water, and don't forget the ice cubes in your drink too—they may not be from a clean source of water. And don't eat uncooked food, like salad, because it may have been washed in dirty water.

Q   I always get badly bitten when I'm away. What do you suggest for that?

DOCTOR   Well, keep your arms and legs covered in the evening when mosquitoes like to bite most of all, and maybe wear a hat too. Insect repellent is very useful but you'll find the most determined mosquito will always find a patch of skin to bite.

Q   And sunstroke?

DOCTOR   Oh, well, obviously the most important thing is not to spend all day in the sun. If you come from a country where you don't get much sunshine, I suggest you spend only about 20 minutes or half an hour in the sun during the first day or two and gradually increase the time. And you should wear a hat, because your head is where you're most likely to catch the sun.

Lesson 10 Reading and Listening, activity 2

WOMAN   OK, here we go, um… question number one: "You're a guest in someone's home, you'd like a cigarette, what do you say?"

MAN   Um… I think it's got to be "a," don't you? "Is it all right if I smoke?"

WOMAN   I think that's most polite, yes. "Is it all right if I smoke?" I'll check that.

MAN   OK, number two: "A friend suggests you have dinner together at a certain restaurant, at the end of the meal the waiter brings the check, what do you say?"

WOMAN   Ooh, um… well…

MAN   Well, it could be "c", because he did offer…

WOMAN   "Your friend suggested dinner", and you expect him to pay.

MAN   … but I think "b" is…

WOMAN   "Let's share this?"

MAN   It's… yeah. Yes. "Let's share this?" He could always persuade you later, couldn't he?

WOMAN   Question number three: "You're visiting a friend when the phone rings, what do you expect her to say to the caller?" Oh, "b."

MAN   I think it has to be "b"

WOMAN   It has to be "b".

MAN   Everything else is very bizarre.

WOMAN   "Would you mind if I called you back, I have a visitor here right now." Yes.

MAN   Uh… number four: "It's late and your neighbors are playing very loud music, what do you say to them?"

WOMAN   "Turn down the music!"

MAN   Yes! No, they're your neighbors, you have to try and get along. I think you'd start with "b."

WOMAN   "Could you turn the music down, please?"

MAN   OK. Five. "You meet someone at a party and get along very well, as she leaves she says, 'Nice meeting you, we must do lunch sometime.'"

WOMAN   Do lunch?

MAN   Do lunch!

WOMAN   Ooh, um… I like "c". "That's a great idea. Bye!"

MAN   But, that sounds like a kiss-off because you don't… she doesn't… you don't know her phone number. It's got to be "b" if you're serious about it.

WOMAN   "b". "Would you mind giving me your phone number?" You're right, "b."

WOMAN   Question number six: "Your host serves you food you don't like (ugh!), you eat it but then the host offers you more, what do you say?"

MAN   It's got to be "a."

WOMAN   It's got to be "a."

MAN   "It was very nice, but no thank you, I've had enough."

WOMAN   Yes.

MAN   Nice and direct, simple, polite.

WOMAN   I think we passed.

MAN   I think so.

Fluency 2 Speaking and Listening, activity 1

1. Oh, how cute. Aren't they just gorgeous! I just want to pick them up and take them home.
2. Well, a picture like this makes me feel really depressed. I mean, well,

what a horrible day. The rain is just pouring down and it's grey and nasty.

3. I look at this picture and I feel really happy. It reminds me of birthdays when I was a child and all the fun we had playing games and all the presents and things.
4. Oh, this is really scary. I wouldn't want to be in this place. It looks really frightening. So dark and gloomy and there's hardly any light. Oh, if I was here, I'd take a cab straight home.
5. Ah. Um, this picture actually makes me feel quite nervous. I've never been very good with heights. I can hardly get up the stairs of my apartment building without feeling a bit dizzy. I certainly couldn't stand here and look down at this view. Uh, no, I'd be really frightened.

Fluency 2 Functions, activity 4

A   I have a ton of work at the moment.
B   Oh, that's too bad.

A   I failed my driving test again.
B   What a shame!

A   I just got a speeding ticket. I was only doing 35!
B   How annoying!

A   Great news! Bill and I are getting married.
B   Congratulations. I'm so happy for you.

A   My teacher thinks I'll never be able to speak Spanish.
B   You're kidding!

A   I've been sick and I think I'll have to quit my job.
B   How terrible!

Fluency 2 Vocabulary and Listening, activity 2

JAN   My name is Jan and I'm from Holland. Um, for me, the color white suggests purity. We wear white for weddings. Black on the other hand means death, we wear black at funerals, and it can also mean bad luck as well. Um, red is, I think danger. Gray, well, gray is a boring color, so dullness.

BISI   I'm from Nigeria and my name is Bisi. In my country white means peace. Black means death, mourning, and unhappiness. And also gray. I remember when I was a child my mother didn't like me wearing it. But it was my favorite color … and she used to say "Why are you wearing that, you look like someone died in the house!" but I liked it. For us, I think green is peace, like white and blue is calmness. Yellow is warmth, like the sun, the sun's rays. Red is danger.

HELENA   I'm Helena from England. To us, if you say someone is yellow that means that they are cowardly. So yellow can mean cowardice. To say that someone is green means they are naive, or inexperienced. Black is the color of death and white, well, purity. Blue can mean sad. We say "Oh, she must be feeling a bit blue today" and of course, blues music is kind of sad. But blue can also mean cold. We say someone is blue with cold. Red is a warmer color and it tends to mean danger, like a red traffic light.

MIGUEL   I'm Miguel from Spain. For us red means passion. Black suggests death and white innocence and purity.

Lesson 11 Listening and Speaking, activity 3

The Stranger, part 1

Francesca was sitting on the front porch swing, drinking iced tea, watching the dust spiral up from under a pickup coming down the country road. The truck was moving slowly, as if the driver were looking for something. It stopped just short of her lane, then turned up it toward the house. Oh God, she thought. Who's this?

She was barefoot, wearing jeans and a faded blue workshirt with the sleeves rolled up, shirttail out. Her hair was fastened up by a tortoiseshell comb her father gave her when she was leaving Italy. She stepped off the porch and walked unhurriedly through the grass toward the gate.

And out of the pickup came Robert Kincaid. He was wearing a tan military-style shirt, and the top three buttons of it were undone. She could see tight chest muscles just below the plain silver chain around his neck. He smiled. "I'm sorry to bother you, but I was looking for a covered bridge out this way, and I can't find it. I think I'm temporarily lost."

Lesson 11 Listening and Speaking, activity 5

The Stranger, part 2

"You're pretty close. The bridge is only about two miles from here." Then Francesca surprised herself by saying, "I'll be glad to show it to you, if you want." He was obviously surprised, slightly, by her offer. But he recovered quickly, and said, "I'd appreciate that. Just take me a minute to make room for you." He was rearranging his gear inside the pickup when the door of the truck swung shut, banging him in the rear. In faded red paint on the green truck door was printed "Kincaid Photography, Bellingham, Washington."

"OK, I think you can squeeze in there now." He held the door, closed it behind her, then went around to the driver's side and got in behind the wheel. He looked at her, just a quick glance, smiled slightly, and said, "Which way?"

"Right." She pointed with her hand.

When they were driving along the lane toward the road, Robert Kincaid pulled a pack of cigarettes from his shirt pocket, shook one halfway out, and offered it to her. For the second time in five minutes, Francesca surprised herself and took one. What am I doing? she thought. He shook out another one, put it between his lips, and flicked a gold Zippo lighter into flame, holding it toward her while he kept his eyes on the road.

They were driving along in silence when Francesca suddenly said, "There it is, just around the curve." The old bridge was red in color, and sat across a small stream.

Robert Kincaid smiled. He quickly looked at her and said, "It's great. A sunrise shot."

Lesson 15 Listening and Speaking, activity 1

Q   Do you mind if I ask you a few questions about table manners, Carlos?

CARLOS No, go right ahead! But I have to tell you, I'm probably not typical!

Q   No problem! So, umm, what do you say at the start of a meal?

CARLOS What do you say at the start of a meal? Oh, I see… "Ahh, this looks good! Let's eat!" Something like that. I mean, it varies, doesn't it?

Q   But you don't say "Enjoy your meal" or anything like that? You know, like the French say "Bon appétit"?

CARLOS No… Only waiters in restaurants say "Enjoy your meal." We sometimes say grace, though, you know, to thank God for the food. Uh-huh. What time do you usually have lunch and dinner?

CARLOS Lunch is right around 12… dinner is about six.

Q   And how long does a typical lunch or dinner last?

CARLOS Lunch is usually about 20 minutes, half an hour… something like that. And dinner is usually a little longer, say 30 or 40 minutes.

Q   That's pretty quick! I mean if you compare it with Mexico or Europe, or…

CARLOS Oh, I know! We eat way too fast here… I mean, if we go to someone's house for a nice evening—and leave the kids with a baby sitter, of course!—then the meal can last much longer… a couple of hours, maybe, 'cause we'll get into the conversation and take our time.

Q   I see… Which hands do you hold your knife and fork in?

CARLOS Oh… when I need to cut something I… umm… let me see… I hold my fork in my right hand usually, but if I need to cut something, I hold my knife in my right hand and my fork in my… uh… left hand, and then put my knife down and switch the fork to my right hand again. I guess that's pretty complicated, isn't it?

Q   Is that typical for Americans?

CARLOS Yeah, I think so, yeah…

Q   Do you use a napkin?

CARLOS Uh-huh.

Q   Where do you usually put it?

CARLOS Oh, sometimes on my lap… usually next to my plate.

Q   And… uh… where do you put your knife and fork after you've finished your meal?

CARLOS On my plate!

Q   I mean, do you put them next to each other, or cross them, or…

CARLOS Yeah, I usually put them quarter of an inch from the edge of the plate… no, I'm kidding! I just throw them on the plate so they don't fall off when I take the plate to the sink! Ah… but, you know, if I was at someone's house or at a nice restaurant, I'd probably take more care, and put them neatly together in the middle of the plate…

Q   Where do you put your hands when you're not actually eating?

CARLOS Not on my lap! Again, if the occasion is semi-formal, then I'd be more conscious of my manners and so forth. But at home I probably put them next to my plate.

Q   Do you ever use your hands to eat at the table, and if so, what kind of food?

CARLOS Oh… fried chicken, pizza, hamburgers, sandwiches, the usual…

Q   What about in a formal setting? At a dinner party, say?

CARLOS Well, I wouldn't serve fried chicken or pizza at a dinner party!

Q   No, I guess not. Umm… when can you smoke during a meal?

CARLOS In our house, never! Otherwise, after the meal, I guess.

Q   And—last question! What do you say and do when someone raises their glass?

CARLOS Well, that looks like an invitation for a toast, so I would wait for them to make the toast, and then raise my glass and drink.

Q   You wouldn't say anything?

CARLOS Oh… I might say "Hear, hear!" or "Well said!"

Q   How about clinking glasses and saying "Cheers!" or "Bottoms up!"?

CARLOS No, that's reserved for when you're drinking for the sake of drinking… at a bar, or if you're trying a special single malt scotch or something… but if you're drinking wine at a dinner party and someone proposes a toast… I wouldn't, no.

Q   OK, well thanks for your help, Carlos.

CARLOS Sure, you're welcome.

Fluency 3 Speaking and Listening, activity 4

TERRY Do you think gender customs in the States have changed over the last 50 years?

BECKY How do you mean?

TERRY Well, for example, do you think men still offer women their seat in a bus if there is nowhere else to sit?

BECKY No, I don't think that I've ever seen that happen. No, I don't think it happens any more.

TERRY What about when a man and a woman are walking on the sidewalk. Does the man walk between the woman and the traffic?

BECKY No, that usually doesn't happen either!

TERRY And do men stand up when a woman comes into the room?

BECKY Well, actually, if it's an older man, uh, then sometimes he will stand up. Yeah, that still happens sometimes

TERRY Do men shake hands with women when they meet?

BECKY I'd say that's about 50-50. I… know if I reach for a man's hand, he will shake my hand.

TERRY And at a dinner table. Do men wait for women to sit down at the table before they sit down? Or doesn't that happen any more?

BECKY I'd say again it depends on whether the man… if it's an older man then yes, but if not, then no.

TERRY OK, and when everyone's sitting down, are women are served first?

BECKY I'd say yes, that usually does happen.

Fluency 3 Reading and Listening, activity 3

CARLA Well, I don't think I agree with this first statement, that the woman in a family should look after the children. I think that that is the responsibility of both parents, the man and the woman. I guess in many homes it's true that it is mainly the woman, but it isn't right that this should be the *rule*. There's no reason why the man shouldn't be the main person caring for the children, as it is in many homes today.

As for the idea that women should not disagree with their husbands, well, that's just ridiculous. Women are entitled to their opinions just as much as men. With any married couple there are always going to be some disagreements. There's no reason why it should always be the woman who gives way.

Men should help with the housework. Definitely.

Married women should work. Hmm. Well, that's more difficult. That's really up to them. If a married woman wants to work, that's her choice. It's more difficult to make a decision if there are children involved, but in principle, I think it's up to the individual woman to choose whether she wants to work or not. For many women it's not a matter or choice but of necessity. They need the money.

Oh, this next one, it is unusual for women not to marry. Well, I'd have to say that that certainly used to be true, but I think now it's becoming more common for women to choose not to marry. Also I think people are marrying later and there are a lot more divorces than there used to be. Certainly a lot of women are choosing to live alone, whether they've been married once or not.

Wives should let their husbands make all major decisions. No, I can't agree with that. Decision making in an ideal marriage should be done jointly between husbands and wives.

And the next one—no, I think that's crazy. I know some women do ignore the fact that their husbands have girlfriends, but the suggestion that they "should" ignore it, that there is some obligation to ignore it is dumb.

A husband should earn more than his wife. Again, I think it's the word "should" that makes me object to this one. Why "should"? There are lots of women who earn more than their husbands, and lots of men who earn more than their wives. That's just the way it is. There's no obligation for one to earn more or less than the other. So I'd have to say a definite no to that one.

And the final one, um, again, I don't think so. It all depends on what arrangement the husband and wife come to. If her job pays better, then it is clearly economically more important to the family than his. But even if it doesn't pay better, or even as well as the man's job, it may be important to her for many other reasons. No, I don't agree with this. One career is not more important than another just because of the gender of the person doing it. Definitely not.

Progress Check 11 – 15 **Sounds, activity 1**

foot play fly fever price fish paper pot finish five page pitch front put

Progress Check 11 – 15 **Sounds, activity 2**

1. ear 2. hair 3. eye 4. hat 5. hate 6. eat 7. art 8. as

Lesson 17 **Listening and Speaking, activity 1**

Part 1

I was on vacation in Connecticut, and I was visiting a church in New Haven. I was sitting in the churchyard, relaxing for a moment, and my bag was beside me, although I was holding the strap. Not the sort of place where you expect anything to happen, is it? Suddenly, someone came up from behind, grabbed my bag and pulled it very hard, breaking the strap. I shouted, first in pain, because when he pulled the bag it hurt my wrist, then in anger as I saw him get on a motorcycle and drive away. I felt awful as I watched my passport, my money, credit cards, various documents disappear down the road. The police were very kind and said that this sort of thing happens too often these days. I thought to myself, "If I ever catch him, I'll kill him!" I told the consulate about the loss of my passport, and I cancelled my credit cards, got some more money, and tried to forget about it. But that wasn't the end of the story.

Lesson 17 **Listening and Speaking, activity 3**

Part 2

Four days later, the police called me at my hotel and said they had some good news. A young man was trying to change some Australian money at the bank in New Haven. Now, there aren't many Australians in Connecticut at this time of year, and secondly, the young man wasn't Australian. So the bank teller called the police, who came very quickly and they stopped the man as he was walking away from the bank. When they questioned him, he broke down and admitted he was guilty. They asked

me to go to the police station to identify him. Well, when he took my bag, I didn't see his face, so I couldn't really say if it was him. But he recognized me, and said, "I'm sorry, I'm really sorry." The police showed me the other things from my bag which he had on him. The man started to cry. The police said he came from New York. He was unemployed and he had a family to look after. I was the victim all right, but now it was me who was feeling sorry.

Lesson 17 **Listening and Speaking, activity 5**

Part 3

The police said "If we let him go, he'll probably take someone else's bag in some other town. But if we send him to court, he'll get a fine, which he won't be able to pay, so he'll go to prison. If he goes to prison, either he'll never take anyone else's bag again, or he'll learn how to do it more efficiently. So what do we do?" I didn't know what to say, so… I just felt so guilty and I had to keep telling myself, "He's the criminal, I'm the victim." Well, in the end, they sent him to court, and he got a fine, which was small enough for him to pay, but now he's got a criminal record, and will probably try to take someone's bag again. It's crazy. He's sorry. I'm sorry. We're all sorry.

Lesson 19 **Reading and Listening, activity 3**

The Umbrella Man, part 2

My mother was staring down at him along the full length of her nose. I wanted to say to her, "Oh, Mom, he's a very old man, and he's polite, and he's in some sort of trouble, so be nice to him." But I didn't say anything.

"I've never forgotten it before," he said.

"You've never forgotten what?" my mother asked.

"My wallet," he said. "I must've left it in my other jacket."

"Are you asking me to give you money?" my mother said.

"No, I'm offering you this umbrella to protect you and to keep, if you would give me a five dollar bill for my cab fare just to get me home."

"Why don't you walk home?" my mother asked.

"Oh, I don't think I could manage it. I've gone too far already."

The idea of getting an umbrella for shelter was very attractive.

"It's a beautiful silk umbrella," the man said. "Why don't you take it, ma'am? It cost me over $30, but that isn't important because I want to get home."

"I don't think it's quite right that I should take an umbrella from you worth $30. I think I'd better just give you the cab fare."

"No, no, no!" he cried. "I would never accept money from you like that! Take the umbrella, dear lady, and keep the rain off your shoulders."

She took out a five dollar bill and gave it to the little man. He took it and gave her the umbrella. He said, "Thank you, ma'am, thank you." Then he was gone.

Lesson 19 **Reading and Listening, activity 5**

The Umbrella Man, part 4

"He went in that door!" It was a bar. The room we were looking into was full of people and cigarette smoke, and our little man was in the middle of it all, without his hat and coat, and moving towards the bar. When he reached it, he spoke to the bartender. The bartender gave him a drink. The little man gave him a five dollar bill. The bartender didn't give him any change. The little man drank it in one gulp.

"That's a very expensive drink," I said.

He was smiling now. He went to where his hat and coat were. He put on his hat. He put on his coat. Then, very quickly, he took from the rack one of the many wet umbrellas, and left.

"Did you see that!" my mother shouted.

"Sssh!" I whispered. "He's coming out."

He didn't see us. He opened his new umbrella and went down the road. We followed him back to the main street where we had first met him, and we watched him as he exchanged his new umbrella for another five dollar bill. This time it was with a tall, thin man who didn't even have a hat or a coat. When it was over he went off again, this time in the opposite direction.

"He never goes to the same bar twice," my mother said. "I guess he's always hoping for rainy days."

Lesson 20 Vocabulary and Listening, activity 2

The Wonderful Pearl, part 2

Wa followed her into the river and for the next three days prepared herbs to cure the Water Spirit's sick daughter. When she had recovered, the Water Spirit thanked Wa and gave her a precious pearl, saying, "This pearl will make every wish come true."

When Wa got back to her village, she heard that while she had been away, the birds had eaten half of the chief's rice. The chief had become very angry, and was looking for her. Tired and hungry, Wa took out the pearl that the Water Spirit had given her, and wished for a house and a bed and a good meal. Suddenly, there in front of her was a beautiful house! She went inside to eat and rest, but while she was eating she heard the chief's son shouting her name. He had heard that she was in the village and had come to punish her. But when he saw her beautiful new house, he looked at her with new respect. "Wa," he stammered, "I w-w-wish to m-m-marry you!"

Wa only laughed. "I hate you. Go away!"

When the young man went home and told his father what Wa had said, the chief was furious. "Get your swords," he shouted to his guards. "We will go and kill that girl!" However, a villager overheard this and ran to warn Wa of the danger. At once, the young girl took out the magic pearl and said, "Pearl, wonderful pearl, protect us from this evil man."

Lesson 20 Sounds

1. She worked long and hard.
2. She jumped up in fear.
3. She'd reached the shore.
4. A scorpion had stung her.
5. He'd heard that she was back.

Fluency 4 Speaking and Listening, activity 3

Q So Pat, you've agreed to answer a few questions for us.

PAT Sure.

Q OK, first of all, you come from the United States, right?

PAT That's right, I was born and raised in Detroit, Michigan.

Q Detroit? Hmm. So, let me ask you, what aspects of your country and culture are you proud of?

PAT Gosh, well... I'm proud that in this country there are so many people from other countries and other cultural and religious backgrounds and that we all, you know, live here in the same country. We're allowed to practice our own religions or cultural, you know, practices that we have and we don't all have to behave or believe the same way.

Q I see. Are there any aspects that you are ashamed of?

PAT Um. That's funny, because what I'm ashamed of is exactly the opposite of what I just said. Because I'm ashamed when people in our country are intolerant of other people's, you know, cultural backgrounds and traditions and other people's religious practices and beliefs.

Q Yeah. Now if you could choose to live anywhere in the world, where would you live?

PAT Gosh. Anywhere in the world. If I could live anywhere in the world... I think actually I'd want to live in this country because I would want to have the freedom to practice and believe, you know, religiously and culturally the way I choose without having that, you know, decided by any sort of government. But I don't know where in this country I'd want to live. I haven't been enough places to make that decision...

Q Well, you can move around...

PAT Yeah, that's good.

Q OK, last question, can you think of five words to describe the most important values and characteristics of your country?

PAT Gosh, the most important values and characteristics... I think well, definitely democracy is one of the words; um, diversity, people from everywhere; um, freedom and let's see... individualism... oh, and I think the most important would be opportunity.

Q Thanks. That's it, Pat. Thank you very much.

PAT Well, you're welcome. Thank you.

Fluency 4 Speaking and Listening, activity 6

RUBEN What do you think about these statements, Gloria, were there any that surprised you?

GLORIA Yeah, I mean, I was surprised by the person who said they kept a gun in the drawer of their night table. I know that a lot of Americans do keep guns, but I guess that still shocks me. I wouldn't keep a gun by my bed.

RUBEN No, I wouldn't either.

GLORIA How about the guy who lets his dog sleep on his bed?

RUBEN I could never do that. I just would not let my dog sleep on the bed.

GLORIA No, nor me. Do you always lock your door when you leave the house?

RUBEN Well, I know I should. And if I'm going out for any length of time, yeah, of course I do, but if I'm just going to the neighbors for something, then sometimes I don't, even though I know I should. Uh, what about you?

GLORIA Oh, yes, I always lock my door. I mean, even if I'm just going to the mailbox, which is right outside my house.

RUBEN That's probably really smart. I think you should always lock your door.

GLORIA Do you watch TV during meals?

RUBEN Usually, yeah. Unless I have guests of course. That would be really rude. But on my own, yes, I do. What about you?

GLORIA Yeah, I do too!

RUBEN Do you think it's OK to visit friends without an invitation?

GLORIA Hmm, that's a hard one. I don't know. If they are very close friends, maybe, but I'd usually call first to ask if it's OK to come over.

RUBEN Yeah, I guess I would too. I don't think I'd ever just show up without any warning.

GLORIA No, I mean, it might be a really inconvenient time for them. Now, Ruben, tell me, when do you wear a suit?

RUBEN Well, hardly ever. I agree with this statement. I hate wearing a suit and I don't wear one except on very formal occasions, you know, like a wedding or something like that. Though I have to say I didn't wear a suit to my own wedding.

GLORIA What? You didn't? What did you wear?

RUBEN I got married in jeans and so did my wife!

GLORIA No way! Wow, I mean I would never have thought that anybody could be that...

Progress Test 1 Lessons 1–10

SECTION 1: VOCABULARY (30 points)

1. a. Match ten of the words in the box with the first ten words in the list. (10 points)

1. alcoholic 2. bad 3. blood 4. parking 5. cassette
6. food 7. guide 8. heart 9. insect 10. military
11. seat 12. department 13. train 14. shoe
15. sleeping 16. public 17. police 18. travel
19. stop 20. wine

```
attack  bite  book  cold  class  drink

hours  house  kit  lot  match  parade

pass  patrol  poisoning  player  pressure

science  terminal  tour
```

alcoholic drink   _____

_____   _____

_____   _____

_____   _____

_____   _____

b. Choose words which go with the other ten words in the list above. Do not use words in the box. Write ten pairs of words. (10 points)

_____   _____

_____   _____

_____   _____

_____   _____

_____   _____

2. Complete these sentences with ten different nouns. (10 points)

Example:
I was sick when I went to Egypt on ___*vacation*___ last year.

1. The principal always makes a short _____ before the graduation ceremony.

2. We have five _____ on each foot.

3. In American English, a _____ is something you turn on and off to control water in a bath or sink.

4. You use _____ to wash yourself with.

5. Pedestrians must not step off the _____ before looking both ways.

6. In my country, you can't feed the animals when you go to a _____ .

7. She's got a _____ because she had too much wine last night.

8. You have to use the stairs when the _____ isn't working.

9. The children had a lot of _____ to play with.

10. A typewriter is a _____ for writing letters with.

Progress Test 1 Lessons 1–10

SECTION 2: GRAMMAR (30 points)

3. a. Choose ten of these words to complete the first ten spaces in the passage. (10 points)

Example:
a) change b) changed c) have changed

1. a) get b) getting c) to get
2. a) for b) from c) since
3. a) has bought b) has built c) has moved
4. a) has lived b) lived c) lives
5. a) her b) him c) them
6. a) found b) given up c) had
7. a) where b) which c) who
8. a) can b) have to c) should
9. a) can b) have c) don't have
10. a) can b) can't c) mustn't

b. Complete the last ten spaces with ten of your own words. (10 points)

Dear Stacey,   December 8th

    Many thanks for your letter and for your news. I hope you're well.
    Lots of things ___have changed___ for me too. My husband and I have decided (1) _____ divorced. We've known each other (2) _____ ten years so it wasn't easy for us. He (3) _____ to a new apartment and now (4) _____ on the other side of the city. The children stay with (5) _____ on Friday and Saturday nights. I've also (6) _____ a job in a liquor store. (A liquor store is a place (7) _____ you can buy alcohol.) My hours are from 11 A.M. to 3 P.M. during the week so I (8) _____ take the children to school every day. Unfortunately I (9) _____ to work Friday and Saturday evenings, too. This means I (10) _____ go out on weekends. My sister sometimes takes care of the children and then (11) _____ can go out during the week.
    I (12) _____ go to work last week because I had food poisoning. I went out for dinner last Monday and I (13) _____ sick all night. The next day I felt terrible and I (14) _____ go to work. I've eaten very little since then and I've (15) _____ a lot of weight. I feel much better now so I (16) _____ back to work yesterday. Have you (17) _____ had food poisoning? It's awful!
    Thanks a lot for the pictures of the baby. Does he look (18) _____ you or your husband? And what's (19) _____ name?
    It's nearly midnight so I have (20) _____ to finish now. It would be great to hear from you again.
                Love,
                Vicky

---

4. Rewrite these sentences. Begin with the words in parentheses. (10 points)

Example: You must not ride a motorbike before you're sixteen. (You can't)
You can't ride a motorbike before you're sixteen.

1. You use it to take photos with. (It's for)
_____

2. We must take some sunscreen. (We have)
_____

3. Can you run five miles? (Are you)
_____

4. You should go to the dentist. (You ought)
_____

5. My throat hurts. (I have)
_____

6. Would you mind telling me the time? (Could you)
_____

7. It's not necessary to wear a helmet. (You don't)
_____

8. Would you like a drink? (Could I)
_____

9. I couldn't read when I was five. (I wasn't)
_____

10. Can you lend me your car this evening? (Can I)
_____

Photocopiable

Progress Test 1 Lessons 1–10

SECTION 3: READING (20 points)

5. Read the passage *Seat Belts, Helmets, and the Law*. What is it mainly about? Choose one of these things. (2 points)

  a. Automobile accidents on highways. ☐

  b. A new law about speed limits. ☐

  c. The cost of not wearing seat belts and helmets. ☐

6. Are these sentences true (T) or false (F) or doesn't the passage say (DS)? (10 points)

  Example: Forty thousand Americans are injured in automobile accidents every year. ☐ *T*

  1. You have to wear a seat belt in the United States. ☐

  2. Hawaii has fewer accidents than any other state. ☐

  3. More than half of U.S. drivers wear a seat belt. ☐

  4. Wearing a seat belt does not increase your chance of surviving a car crash. ☐

  5. The average hospital cost for drivers who were not wearing a seat belt was $9,004. ☐

  6. If you are wearing a seat belt in an accident, your hospital bill will probably be less than if you are not wearing one. ☐

  7. Most motorcycle riders wear a helmet. ☐

  8. In most states, police officers can stop you if you are not wearing a seat belt. ☐

  9. In states where the police can stop and fine drivers for not wearing a seat belt, most people wear seat belts. ☐

  10. You have to wear a helmet everywhere in the United States. ☐

7. Why is it a good idea to wear a seat belt, according to the passage? Make notes. Use no more than 40 words. (8 points)

_____

_____

_____

_____

_____

SEAT BELTS, HELMETS, AND THE LAW

Currently, about 40,000 Americans die each year in highway crashes, and hundreds of thousands more are seriously and sometimes permanently injured as a result of automobile accidents. These accidents cost the taxpayer approximately $137 billion every year. As doctors and safety experts have said for years, many of the more serious injuries are unnecessary and only happen because drivers do not follow the seat belts laws.

A recent Department of Transportation report analyzed 879,670 auto accidents and 10,353 motorcycle crashes in seven states (Hawaii, Maine, Missouri, New York, Pennsylvania, Utah, and Wisconsin) since 1990. It found:

- Only about 67% of U.S. motorists use seat belts.
- About 60% of motorists who die would live if they used seat belts.
- Wearing a seat belt decreases hospitalization costs by an average of nearly $5,000 per patient.
- Motorcyclists who do not wear helmets are more than three times as likely to have brain injuries as those who do.
- Motorcyclists who do not wear helmets and have brain injuries have hospital costs averaging more than $14,000 each.

The average hospital cost for drivers who were not wearing a seat belt was $13,937, compared with $9,004 for drivers who were. Private insurance paid for 69% of the hospital cost but taxpayers paid the rest. Among motorcyclists, the average hospital cost for riders who wore helmets was $14,377, which is less than the $15,578 average for those who did not.

So why don't more people follow the law? Ten states have primary seat belt laws, which allow police officers to stop and fine drivers and passengers for not wearing seat belts. These laws increase seat belt use by 15%, experts say. Thirty-nine states have less effective secondary laws, which allow officers to give fines only when stopping drivers for other reasons. Twenty-five states, the District of Columbia, and Puerto Rico have laws requiring motorcyclists to wear helmets.

Adapted from "Report: seat belts, helmets save lives and health costs" by Christina Kent, *American Medical News*, March 4, 1996.

Progress Test 1 Lessons 1–10

SECTION 4: WRITING (20 points)

8. Imagine that you have gone to see the doctor because you are not feeling well. Write the conversation between the doctor and yourself. For example, talk about the medical problems you have had, explain your current condition, give the doctor's advice. Write 10 to 15 sentences.

Photocopiable

Progress Test 2   Lessons 11–20

SECTION 1: VOCABULARY (30 points)

1. a. Underline the word which doesn't belong and leave a group of three related words. (5 points)

   b. Add one other word to the groups of words. (5 points)

Example:
burglar friend <u>mugging</u> musician *victim*

1. east north south toast _____

2. cup bowl saucer spoon _____

3. fall spring storm summer _____

4. dry fog ice snow _____

5. did drunk eaten written _____

2. a. Underline five words or phrases you can put with *do*. (5 points)

a cake a decision a mistake a noise a phone call

an appointment business friends harm

notes someone a favor the bed the dishes

the tea your best

   b. Write five other words or phrases you can put with *do*. (5 points)

_____

_____

_____

_____

_____

3. Complete the sentences with ten different particles. (10 points)

Example: He took ___*out*___ a pen and wrote his name.

1. He put his coat _____ because it was cold.

2. He got _____ his car to get out of the rain.

3. Can you turn the radio _____ a bit? It's too loud.

4. The vacuum cleaner isn't plugged _____ .

5. We'll take care _____ your cat when you're on vacation.

6. Who are you going to vote _____ in the next election?

7. I asked her for the stamp, but she'd already thrown the envelope _____ .

8. I've never been able to give _____ smoking.

9. The children waved _____ their grandmother.

10. You can't watch TV. I've turned it _____ .

Progress Test 2 Lessons 11–20

SECTION 2: GRAMMAR (30 points)

4. a. Choose ten of these words to complete the first ten spaces in the passage. (10 points)

Example: a) although b) but c) however

1. a) danger b) dangerous c) dangerously

2. a) has b) had c) was

3. a) had laughed b) laughed c) were laughing

4. a) bad b) good c) well

5. a) never b) often c) sometimes

6. a) stay b) stayed c) were staying

7. a) understanding b) understand c) understood

8. a) am b) were c) would

9. a) can b) might b) won't

10. a) he b) I c) they

b. Complete the last ten spaces with ten of your own words. (10 points)

Foreign drivers aren't always welcome in Britain, _although_ most of them are very good drivers. However, tourist Graziano Montironi is warning British motorists that he's (1) _____ . Graziano, on vacation, with his wife, Lucia, and their three young children, reached York in the north of England yesterday afternoon.

Forty-year-old Graziano, a truck driver from Rome, (2) _____ just arrived in York in his car when heads there started to turn. People (3) _____ when they saw the signs in his car: "Sorry, I'm Italian and I'm a (4) _____ driver. Keep a safe distance. I drive dangerously. We don't want an accident."

Graziano said yesterday: "It's the first time I've been to England, so I've (5) _____ driven on the left. While we (6) _____ in a bed and breakfast in Dover, I explained this to one of the other guests. He was American so he (7) _____ my problem. 'If I (8) _____ you, I'd put some stickers in your windows. That (9) _____ help,' he said and that's what (10) _____ did. Italians (11) _____ known as bad drivers and I'm not too proud to admit it.

Anyway, it's my wife's car. She (12) _____ drive in England because she's too nervous. If we (13) _____ an accident, it will be my fault. So I want (14) _____ make sure nothing happens."

A motorist who pulled up behind Graziano's car said, "I was going down Tower Street (15) _____ it suddenly pulled out in front (16) _____ me

from the left. Fortunately, I (17) _____ hit him. I read what the driver (18) _____ written on his stickers and gave him enough room. I'd probably do the same if I (19) _____ to Italy. It seems like a (20) _____ idea!"

5. Rewrite these sentences. Begin with the words in brackets. (10 points)

Example:
They speak English and French in Canada. (English)
English and French are spoken in Canada.

1. I was drying some shirts when one of them caught fire. (While)

   _____

2. It's been too rainy recently. (There's)

   _____

3. If you don't give that pen to me, I'll take it from you. (I'll)

   _____

4. We like pasta, but we don't have it every day. (Although)

   _____

5. They set out when they'd listened to the weather forecast. (After)

   _____

6. You use money for buying things. (Money)

   _____

7. There isn't enough wind to go hang gliding. (It)

   _____

8. It might not be very sunny tomorrow. (There)

   _____

9. When I plugged the computer in, it exploded. (The computer)

   _____

10. I wouldn't work if I didn't have to. (If)

   _____

Photocopiable

Progress Test 2 Lessons 11–20

SECTION 3: READING (20 points)

6. Read *Dreamtime*. There are five paragraphs in the text. Which paragraphs describe these things? Write the number of the paragraph in the box. (6 points)

a. Aboriginal lifestyle. ☐

b. Aboriginal life since 1778. ☐

c. Aboriginal religious ceremonies. ☐

7. Are these sentences true (T) or false (F) or doesn't the passage say (DS)? (9 points)

Example:
There are fewer than 30,000 Aborigines today. ☐ *DS*

1. The Aboriginal culture is older than Middle Eastern culture. ☐

2. When the Europeans arrived, most Aborigines lived on the coast. ☐

3. Aborigine groups always lived in the same place. ☐

4. The Aboriginal lifestyle today is the same as it has always been. ☐

5. *Didgeridoos* are important religious celebrations. ☐

6. Women take part in the religious ceremonies. ☐

7. Aborigines' bodies are painted before the *corroboree* ceremonies begin. ☐

8. *Corroborees* can mark important events in an Aborigine's life. ☐

9. Aborigines believe in their own connection with the past and the future. ☐

8. Why were animals and plants important to the Aborigines? Make notes. (5 points)

_____

_____

_____

_____

_____

_____

Dreamtime

1 THE AUSTRALIAN CONTINENT had its own culture, which was rich and complex in its customs, religions, and lifestyles, long before the ancient civilizations in the Middle East, Europe, and the Americas developed. For more than 40,000 years before European navigators visited their coast, the Australian Aborigines had lived on this continent. It is estimated that before the arrival of the first European settlers in 1778, the Aborigine population was more than 300,000. At that time, 500 different languages were spoken.

2 The Aborigines lived in groups of 10 to 50 people. They lived a mostly peaceful, nomadic life, moving from one area to another in their search for food. They collected fruit, nuts, and insects to eat and hunted kangaroos and emus. They adapted to the harsh environment; they were perfectly at home before white settlers arrived.

3 The older men in the group had to build the group's identity through its religious beliefs and traditions. These developed in close harmony with their environment and were very important to the group members. The idea of Dreamtime or Dreaming was very important in their way of life. This is the time of the creation, when the land, sea, sky, and all creatures were made. Dreamtime is a time that existed long ago, although for Aborigines it is an experience which links the past, the present, and the future. The Aborigines believed that a person's spirit did not die when the person died. Instead, these spirits—of their parents and grandparents—continued to live on, in rocks, animals, plants, or other human forms. So each group formed a special relationship with an animal or a plant, which acted as a symbol of their group identity and as a protector. Rock paintings were of special importance and record Aboriginal beliefs. These are also passed on from parents to their children by storytelling and through song and dance.

4 Although the Aboriginal population of Australia is greatly reduced today, some of their customs live on. The ceremony of celebrating with song and dance is called *corroboree*. The dancers wear special clothes and body paint. They are accompanied by drums and other instruments, and *didgeridoos*, hollow pieces of wood producing a strange sound which is said to sound like the calling of the spirits of their ancestors. *Corroborees* are sometimes performed to persuade the spirits to bring rain, or to provide successful hunting. Other *corroborees* are held to mark the time when boys reach manhood, to mourn death, or to celebrate love.

5 With the arrival of the European settlers, the way of life of the Aborigines changed dramatically. Thousands died from European diseases and many had to leave their lands. The Aboriginal culture had prepared the people for everything they might expect to face in life—everything, that is, except white settlers.

Progress Test 2 Lessons 11–20

SECTION 4: WRITING (20 points)

9. Think about an interesting day you have had recently. Describe what happened. Try to use a variety of different structures. Write 10 to 15 sentences. (20 points)

_____

_____

_____

_____

_____

_____

_____

_____

_____

_____

_____

_____

_____

_____

_____

_____

_____

_____

_____

_____

_____

_____

Answers Progress Test 1 Lessons 1–10

SECTION 1: VOCABULARY [30 points]

1. a. (10 points: 1 point for each correct answer.)

1. drink	6. poisoning
2. cold	7. book
3. pressure	8. attack
4. lot	9. bite
5. player	10. parade

b. (10 points: 1 point for each appropriate answer.)
Possible Answers

11. belt	16. school
12. store	17. officer
13. station	18. agent
14. polish	19. lights
15. bag	20. glass

2. (10 points: 1 point for each appropriate answer.)

1. speech	6. zoo
2. toes	7. hangover
3. faucet	8. elevator
4. soap	9. toys
5. sidewalk	10. machine

SECTION 2: GRAMMAR [30 points]

3. a. (10 points: 1 point for each correct answer.)

1. c) to get	6. a) found
2. a) for	7. a) where
3. c) has moved	8. a) can
4. c) lives	9. b) have
5. b) him	10. b) can't

b. (10 points: 1 point for each appropriate answer.)

11. I	16. went
12. didn't	17. ever
13. felt / was	18. like
14. didn't	19. his
15. lost	20. got

4. (10 points: 1 point for each correct sentence.)
1. It's for taking photos with.
2. We have to take some sunscreen.
3. Are you able to run five miles?
4. You ought to go to the dentist.
5. I have a sore throat.
6. Could you tell me the time?
7. You don't have to wear a helmet.
8. Could I get you a drink?
9. I wasn't able to read when I was five.
10. Can I borrow your car this evening?

SECTION 3: READING [20 points]

5. (2 points)

c

6. (10 points: 1 point for each correct answer.)

1. T	6. T
2. DS	7. DS
3. T	8. F
4. F	9. T
5. F	10. F

7. (8 points: 2 points for each of the four things.)
(1) You might live through a car crash.
(2) A seat belt decreases your hospitalization cost.
(3) You might get fined.
(4) Taxpayers have to pay for some people's hospitalization.

SECTION 4: WRITING [20 points]

8. (20 points)
Tell students what you will take into consideration when grading their written work. Criteria should include:
– efficient communication of meaning (7 points)
– grammatical accuracy (7 points)
– coherence in the ordering or the information or ideas (3 points)
– layout, capitalization, and punctuation (3 points)

It is probably better not to use a rigid grading system with the written part of the test. If, for example, you always deduct a point for a grammatical mistake, you may find that you are over-penalizing students who write a lot or who take risks. Deduct points if students haven't written the minimum number of sentences stated in the test.

Answers Progress Test 2 Lessons 11–20

SECTION 1: VOCABULARY [30 points]

1. a. (5 points: 1 point for each correct answer.)
1. toast
2. spoon
3. storm
4. dry
5. did

b. (5 points: 1 point for each appropriate answer.)
1. west
2. plate
3. winter
4. any noun associated with weather, e.g. rain, wind
5. any past participle, e.g. finished, said

2. a. (5 points: 1 point for each correct answer.)
business
harm
someone a favor
the dishes
your best

b. (5 points: 1 point for each appropriate answer.)
Possible Answers

well	the shopping
your homework	damage
the housework	the ironing

3. (10 points: 1 point for each correct answer.)

1.	on	6.	for
2.	into	7.	away
3.	down	8.	up
4.	in	9.	to
5.	of	10.	off

SECTION 2: GRAMMAR [30 points]

4. a. (10 points: 1 point for each correct answer.)

1.	b) dangerous	6.	c) were staying
2.	b) had	7.	c) understood
3.	b) laughed	8.	b) were
4.	a) bad	9.	b) might
5.	a) never	10.	b) I

b. (10 points: 1 point for each appropriate answer.)

11.	are	16.	of
12.	doesn't	17.	didn't
13.	have	18.	had
14.	to	19.	went
15.	when	20.	good

5. (10 points: 1 point for each correct sentence.)
1. While I was drying some shirts, one of them caught fire.
2. There's been too much rain recently.
3. I'll take that pen from you if you don't give it to me.
4. Although we like pasta, we don't have it every day.
5. After they'd listened to the weather forecast, they set out.
6. Money is used for buying things.
7. It isn't windy enough to go hang gliding.
8. There might not be much sun tomorrow.
9. The computer exploded when I plugged it in.
10. If I didn't have to work, I wouldn't.

SECTION 3: READING [20 points]

6. (6 points)
a. Paragraph 2
b. Paragraph 5
c. Paragraph 3 and 4

7. (9 points: 1 point for each correct answer.)

1.	T	4.	F	7.	T
2.	DS	5.	F	8.	T
3.	F	6.	DS	9.	T

8. (5 points: 1 point for each of these five things.)
(1) They gathered fruit, nuts, and insects to eat (2) and hunted kangaroos and emus. (3) They moved from one area to another in their search for food. (4) Their ancestors' spirits lived on after death, sometimes in animals and plants. (5) Totems, which protected and gave groups their identity, were usually animals or plants.

SECTION 4: WRITING [20 points]

9. (20 points)
Tell students what you will take into consideration when grading their written work. Criteria should include:
– efficient communication of meaning (7 points)
– grammatical accuracy (7 points)
– coherence in the ordering or the information or ideas (3 points)
– layout, capitalization, and punctuation (3 points)

It is probably better not to use a rigid grading system with the written part of the test. If, for example, you always deduct a point for a grammatical mistake, you may find that you are over-penalizing students who write a lot or who take risks. Deduct points if students haven't written the minimum number of sentences stated in the test.

Photocopiable

Practice Book Answer Key

Lesson 1

VOCABULARY
1. Across: chest, arm, head, toe, throat, knee, lip, chin, waist
   Down: calf, face, heel, eyes, ear, ankle, thigh
2. bald, big, brown, fat, long, slim
3. bald: head
   big: head toe lip eyes ear thigh
   brown: eyes
   fat: lip face ankle thigh
   long: arm throat chin calf face thigh
   slim: calf thigh waist face ankle
4. I've got two: arms, legs, heels, eyes, calves, knees, thighs, ankles, ears, elbows, feet, lips, shoulders, thumbs, wrists.

GRAMMAR
1. 1. No, I haven't. I left school when I was sixteen.
   2. No, I haven't. I don't like acting.
   3. Yes, and I've played too.
   4. Yes, I had an appointment last week.
   5. Yes, I have. But I'm divorced now.
   6. No, I haven't. I prefer classical music.
2.

infinitive	**past simple**	**past participle**
become	became	become
break	broke	broken
drink	drank	drunk
drive	drove	driven
eat	ate	eaten
pay	paid	paid
run	ran	run
say	said	said
speak	spoke	spoken
teach	taught	taught
wear	wore	worn

3. 1. eaten 2. broken 3. drunk
   4. spoken 5. run 6. driven
6. 1. Did 2. Has 3. Have
   4. Did 5. Did 6. Has

READING AND WRITING
1. *Possible Answers*
   1. Are you fit?
   2. Have you ever cut yourself badly?
   3. Have you ever had a bad cough?
   4. Have you ever given up something because of your health?
   5. Have you ever been ill on vacation?
   6. Have you ever had a car crash/been to the hospital?

Lesson 2

GRAMMAR
1. 1. 's 2. 've 3. 's 4. 've
   5. 've 6. 've
2. 1. 've 2. – 3. 's 4. – 5. 've
   6. 've
3. feel give go hear know leave meet read see speak take think
4. felt heard left met read thought
5. 1. died 2. had 3. have lost
   4. have/known
   5. have/visited/went 6. was
   7. did/change 8. has stayed
6. *Possible Answers*
   1. He's bought an apartment.
   2. He hasn't changed jobs.
   3. He hasn't gotten married.
   4. He hasn't moved to his new apartment.
   5. He's taken some exams.
   6. He's visited Jamaica.

READING
1. 1. job 2. baby 3. driving test
   4. smoking 5. apartment

Lesson 3

VOCABULARY
1. 1. parade 2. soldiers
   3. vacation 4. celebrate
   5. speech 6. fireworks

GRAMMAR
3. 1. have known 2. have celebrated 3. have not sent
   4. have not had 5. has been
   6. have not ridden 7. has worked 8. have you played

READING
1. love letters: First sent by a French duke in 1415.
   a fertility festival: There was a Roman festival on February 14th called Lupercalia.
   the saint of lovers: He is St. Valentine.
   the third century: This is when St. Valentine was killed.
   February 14th: This is St Valentine's Day.
3. a: paragraph 2 b: paragraph 4
   c: paragraph 1
   d: paragraph 3 e: paragraph 5

Lesson 4

GRAMMAR
1. 1. gives money to bank customers.
   2. carries your suitcases to your hotel room.
   3. sells alcohol and wine.
   4. is in the first year of high school.
   5. you put bags of garbage.
   6. means "no parking".

2. 1, 3, 5, 6
3. 1. which 2. which 3. who
   4. which 5. which 6. who
4. 1. who 2. which 3. which
   4. where 5. who 6. where

VOCABULARY
1.

US	**GB**
french fries	chips
subway	underground
closet	cupboard
first floor	ground floor
gasoline	petrol
to call collect	to make a reverse charge call
drugstore	chemist's
eggplant	aubergine
elevator	lift
to stand in line	to queue
movie	film
garbage	rubbish
one-way ticket	single ticket
round-trip ticket	return ticket
truck	lorry
candy	sweets/chocolate

2. 1. movie, stand in line
   2. call collect 3. elevator
   4. subway 5. truck
3. American: 1 2 5 8
   British: 3 4 6 7
4. 3. pants; closet 4. gas
   6. drugstore 7. stood in line; movie

Lesson 5

VOCABULARY AND READING
1. A: flat light round soft small wool
   B: big flat hard heavy leather metal oblong
   C: curved flat glass hard oval small wood
   D: flat long metal plastic thin
2. 1. B 2. A 3. C
3. It's made of metal and plastic. It's long, thin, and flat.

GRAMMAR
1. 1. What does it look like?
   2. Is it soft or hard?
   3. What's it made of?
   4. What does it feel like?
   5. Is it very big?
   6. How much does it weigh?
3. 1. knife 2. mirror 3. hat
   4. briefcase
4. 1. A knife is for cutting things.
   2. To look at yourself, you use a mirror.
   3. A hat is for keeping your head warm.
   4. To carry things, you use a briefcase.
5. *Possible Answers*
   1. A comb is for combing your hair.
   2. A notepad is for writing notes on.
   3. A credit card is for paying for things.
   4. A towel is for drying yourself with.
   5. A tent is for sleeping in.
   6. A wallet is for carrying money in.
6. 1. 60 2. 56, 57 3. 58 4. 7

READING AND WRITING
1. 1. c 2. a 3. a
2. rattle 3 b overalls 2 b wash cloth 2 c down jacket 1 b oven cleaner 3 c trunk 1 a
3. *Example definition*
   "Stroller": a chair on wheels used for carrying babies or children who are too young to walk.

Lesson 6

GRAMMAR
1. 1 3 4 5 6 2
2. 1. e 2. d 3. f 4. c 5. b
   6. a
3. 1. have to 2. don't have to
   3. doesn't have to 4. have to
   5. don't have to 6. has to

VOCABULARY AND READING
2. The words in the text are:
   curve gas pedal stop sign test turn signals
3. 1. F 2. F 3. F 4. T 5. F 6. T
   7. T 8. T

Lesson 7

VOCABULARY
1. 1. locked 2. climbed
   3. shouted 4. waved
   5. whispered
3. a parent 4; a teacher 1; a driver 2; an astronaut 6; an interpreter 5; a student 3
4. Across: drink use stand play draw ride climb read make speak see
   Down: touch run drive sleep

GRAMMAR
1. 1. can/can't stand
   2. could/couldn't speak
   3. can/can't drive
   4. could/couldn't draw
   5. can/can't drink
   6. could/couldn't climb
   7. can/can't see
   8. could/couldn't play
   9. can/can't touch
3. 1. can't 2. can 3. can't
   4. can 5. can't 6. can't

Lesson 8

READING AND WRITING
1. 1. F 2. T 3. F 4. T 5. F
   6. T 7. T 8. F 9. F 10. F
   11. T 12. F 13. F 14. F
   15. T 16. T 17. T 18. T
   19. T 20. F 21. T 22. F
   23. T 24. F 25. T

GRAMMAR
2. 1. You can't smoke. 2. You can't take food or drink into the store. 3. You can ride a bike here. 4. You can park here if you are disabled.
   5. You can't park here. 6. You can't driver faster than 65 mph.
5. *Possible Answers*
   1. Can I go home now?
   2. Can I eat these?
   3. Can I walk there?
   4. Can I borrow a few books?
   5. Can I go out tonight?

VOCABULARY
1. 1. at a zoo 2. in a library
   3. in an airplane 4. in a museum

Lesson 9

VOCABULARY
1. high sick sore thirsty tired
2. I'm: sick/thirsty/tired
   My ear/leg hurts.
   I have a/an earache/ hangover/headache/sore throat/fever.
   I have the flu/high blood pressure/jet lag/ sunstroke/toothache.
3. Dialogue 1: The woman has a headache.
   Dialogue 2: The man has the flu.
4. 1. d 2. b 3. c 4. a
5. Dialogue 1: take an aspirin
   Dialogue 2: go home to bed

GRAMMAR
1. ?Dialogue 1: The woman should/ought to take two aspirin.
   Dialogue 2: The man should/ought to go home to bed.
3. 1. You shouldn't smoke.
   2. You should get plenty of exercise.
   3. You shouldn't go to bed late.
   4. You should eat plenty of fresh fruit and vegetables.
   5. You should learn to relax.
4. 1. (✗) 2. (✓) 3. (✓) 4. (✗)

READING AND WRITING
2. 1. The most popular sports in North America are baseball and football.
   2. The spectators are Americans from every income and ethnic group.
   3. The baseball season is spring and summer.
   4. The football season is fall and winter.
   5. They are important because

alumni (ex-students) give money to their old school; they give more if the college has a winning team.

Lesson 10

READING AND FUNCTIONS
1. c f a d g e b
2. Dialogue 2: Of course you can! Will you be eating here?
   Dialogue 3: It's on the shelf by the front door.
3. 1. What is the situation?
   Dialogue 1: asking for directions
   Dialogue 2: asking to use the phone
   Dialogue 3: asking for permission to bring a friend home
   2.
   Dialogue 1: strangers
   Dialogue 2: know each other
   Dialogue 3:family
   3.
   Dialogue 1: in the street
   Dialogue 2: in someone's house
   Dialogue 3: at home
4. 1. asks someone for something: Can you tell me how to get to the bus station?
   Could I have a ride?
   2. offers to do something: Do you want me to pick something up on the way home?
   3. asks for permission: Could I use your phone, please?
   Can I bring a college friend home this evening?

GRAMMAR
1. 1. (✓) 2. (✓) 3. (✗) 4. (✗) 5. (✓)
3. *Possible Answers*
   1. I'll answer it.
   2. Can I get you some?
   3. I'll make it.
   4. Could I do it for you?
   5. Would you like me to?
   6. I'll help you look for them.
4. *Possible Answers*
   1. Could you open the door, please?
   2. Can I have that magazine?
   3. Can I help you?

Lesson 11

READING
1. 4. His father heard a ghost.
2. three o'clock
   at three o'clock: His mother and father twice heard a ghost that sounded like Ben at 3:00 in the morning of December 14th.
   at six o'clock: Ben arrived home at 6:00 in the morning after a Christmas party.
   at ten o'clock: Ben's father woke him up at 10:00 A.M.
3. *Possible Answers*
   1. ...his parents heard voices in

the garden.
   2. ...they heard Ben's voice in the garden.
   3. ...his parents heard voices downstairs.
   4. ...Ben said he got home at 6:00 A.M.
   5. ...the noise stopped.

GRAMMAR
1. 1. She was having breakfast at eight o'clock.
   2. She was getting into her car at a quarter to nine.
   3. She was having a cup of coffee at a quarter past eleven.
   4. She was talking on the phone at five o'clock.
   5. She was playing tennis at a quarter past seven.
   6. She was ironing her clothes at half past ten.
3. 1. I was crossing the road when the car hit me.
   2. I was watching TV when there was a power cut.
   3. I was recording a film when the VCR broke down.
   4. I was running in a race when I hurt my ankle.
   5. I was getting some money when the gunman came into the bank.
   6. I was skiing without a hat when it started to snow.

VOCABULARY
1. closing time insect bite jet lag military service mobile phone musical instrument police officer roast chicken sleeping bag speed limit
2. *Possible Answers*
   1. art gallery 2. work shirt
   3. cheese sandwich
   4. guidebook 5. railroad station 6. single room

Lesson 12

VOCABULARY
1. *Possible Answers*
   experience: nice, pen, rice, peer, price
   cottage: tea, age, goat, coat, cage
   lampposts: map(s), stamp(s), stop(s), pop(s), most, slam
2. nouns: bark, bush, sidewalk
   adjectives: confused, heavy, old–fashioned, strange
   verbs: bark, vanish
3. 1. heavy 2. barking
   3. sidewalk 4. old–fashioned
   5. confused 6. vanished

GRAMMAR
1. 1. While we were standing outside the church, it started to rain.
   2. While the police officer was taking notes, the thieves ran away.
   3. While their mother was working, the children stayed at school.
   4. While I was having lunch,

my cousins arrived.
   5. While he was taking a shower, the telephone rang.
   6. While we were climbing the mountain, my cousin broke her arm.
2. 1. We opened up our umbrellas and ran to the car.
   2. She ran after them and caught one of them. The other one got away.
   3. She picked them up at about five o'clock when she left the office.
   4. I asked them if they would like something to eat.
   5. It stopped ringing before he could get to it.
   6. A helicopter took her to the hospital.
3. 1. While they were traveling in Asia, they heard the news.
   2. She came to my office while I was speaking on the phone.
   3. While he was playing tennis, he got sunstroke.
   4. He scored his first goal while he was playing against his old team.
5. 1. I got home 2. her father died 3. I sat down 4. I went to the museum 5. the lights went out 6. she arrived
6. 1. was working 2. wanted 3. remembered 4. knew 5. packed 6. prepared 7. drew 8. was working 9. stopped 10. saw 11. was painting 12. said

Lesson 13

VOCABULARY
1. 1. clean 2. wet 3. more 4. flat 5. rich 6. noisy

GRAMMAR
1. 1. hot 2. hilly 3. industrial 4. peaceful 5. rainy
2. 1. hot 2. hills 3. industry 4. peaceful 5. rain
3. 1. There isn't enough heat in our house in winter.
   2. It's too hilly for cyclists.
   3. The town isn't industrial enough.
   4. There isn't enough peace for the baby to sleep.
   5. It's too rainy to go out for a walk.
4. 1. There aren't enough
   2. There's too much 3. There are too many 4. There's too much 5. There isn't enough 6. There are too many
6. 1. There are fewer theaters than movie theaters in the United States.
   2. There is less industry in the south than in the north.
   3. There is less crime in the country than in the big cities.
   4. There were fewer freeways twenty years ago than there are today.
   5. There is less rain in summer than in winter.

READING AND WRITING

1. 1. T 2. C 3. T 4. C 5. T
   6. T 7. C 8. C
3. 2
4. the most: 3; the least: 1

Lesson 14

GRAMMAR

1. build–built   eat–eaten
   hold–held   know–known
   put–put   write–written
2. 1. is known   2. is called
   3. .is celebrated   4. are put
   5. were not allowed
3. 1. are decorated   2. are closed
   3. eat   4. are sold
   5. exchange   6. are held
4. 1. Easter buns are called "hot
   cross buns."
   2. Hot cross buns are eaten on
   Good Friday.
   3 The buns are made with
   dried fruit.
   4. The buns are marked with a
   cross before they are baked.
   5. The buns are toasted before
   they are eaten.
   6. The buns are served with
   butter.

Lesson 15

GRAMMAR

1. 1. although I use it when I
   make desserts.
   2. we eat out about once a week.
   3. but we usually drink from
   mugs.
   4. although we usually have it
   as a main course.
   5. but I always have a good
   dinner.
   6. although I like toast
   occasionally.
2. 1. Although I like chocolate a
   lot, I try to have only one piece
   a day.
   2. I have a sweet tooth but I try
   not to put too much sugar in
   my coffee.
   3. I like salad with meat or fish
   although my husband prefers
   cooked vegetables.
   4. We have a light breakfast
   during the week. However, we
   have a large brunch on Sundays.
   5. We like pasta a lot, but we
   don't have it very often.

VOCABULARY AND WRITING

1. bowl fork napkin
   spoon glass plate knife
   table cloth
2. the woman: fish, potatoes,
   peas, bread
   the man: steak, french fries,
   salad, bread

Lesson 16

GRAMMAR

1. 1. so   2. because   3. because
   4. so   5. because   6. so

VOCABULARY

1. 1. nouns: flood   hurricane
   rain   storm   thunder   wind
   adjectives: wet
   2. nouns: frost   ice   snow
   adjectives: freezing
   3. nouns: sun   wind
   adjectives: changeable   dry
   mild
2. *Possible Answers*
   sun dry hot shine clear
   sunny

READING AND WRITING

1. warm clear sunny highs
   lows rain snow cold
   temperature cloudy showers
   thunderclouds heavy rain
   lightning
2. B
3. 1. F   2. T   3. F
   4. T   5. T   6. F

Lesson 17

READING

1. a flood
2. a 2   b 5   c 3   d 4   e 1

GRAMMAR

1. 1. I leave   2. we listen
   3. they'll learn   4. I lose
   5. we like   6. they'll look
2. 1. do / will be   2. fail / won't
   be able   3. don't have / will
   buy   4. don't get / will wait
   5. drink / will ... feel
   6. is / won't go

VOCABULARY AND WRITING

1. 1. injured / dangerous
   2. mugger / gun
   3. turn off / gas, electricity /
   unplug
3. 1, 2, 3, 5, 6
4. *Possible Answers*
   2. If you don't go to a window,
   nobody will see you.
   3. If you get down on your
   hands and knees, there will be
   less smoke.
   4. If you try to get your
   valuables, you may get burned.
   5. If you call 911, the
   firefighters will come.
   6. If you wait for the fire
   department, you can explain
   what happened.

Lesson 18

VOCABULARY

1. 1. novel   2. dog   3. juice
   4. pen   5. telephone   6. soap

GRAMMAR

1. 1. Which place would you go to?
   2. Why would you choose that
   one?
   3. When would you go?
   4. Who would you take with
   you?
   5. How would you spend your
   vacation?

READING AND WRITING

1. *Possible Answers*
   1. Which books would you
   read?
   2. What kind of music would
   you listen to?
   3. What would you watch on
   television?
   4. Would you send any
   postcards?
   5. Would you get any exercise?
   6. What would you miss?

Lesson 19

GRAMMAR

1. 1. I'd travel   2. we do   3. I'd
   take   4. I'd dance   5. you
   drive   6. they'd tell
2. 1. went / would take   2. was
   or were / would go   3. met /
   would tell   4. left / would
   borrow   5. would help /
   wanted   6. would try / offered

Lesson 20

GRAMMAR AND READING

1. e   d   a   c   b
2. 1. would   2. had   3. had
   4. would   5. had   6. had
   7. had   8. would
3. 1. I'd cut   3. She'd   6. He'd
4. 1. our friends had already left
   2. her brother had become ill
   3. I had tried them on
   4. the guard blew his whistle
   5. The party had started
   6. I saw the dog
5. 1. left   2. seen   3. gone
   4. died   5. flown   6. lived
6. 1. decided   2. had chosen
   3. made   4. asked   5. had
   been   6. found   7. had arrived
   8. hadn't taken